Sales Playbooks

CORY BRAY AND HILMON SOREY

Copyright © 2019 Cory Bray and Hilmon Sorey
All rights reserved.

ISBN 13: 9781798257296

CONTENTS

Chapter 1: Introduction 1
    What Is a Sales Playbook? 2
    When to Build a Sales Playbook? 4
    Impact on Onboarding and Retention 5
    Impact on Channel Partners 6
    Triangle Selling™ 6
    How to Use This Book 8

Part 1: Preparing to Develop the Playbook 11
Chapter 2 Element: Gathering Information 13
    Step One: Specific Information You Will Need 13
    Pro Tip: Rationale for Some Assets 14
    Step Two: Making the Request 15
    Step Three: Tracking Assets and Following Up 16
    Take Action 16
    Traps to Avoid 17

Chapter 3 Element: Interviews 18
    Step One: Preparing for Interviews 18
    Pro Tip 19
    Step Two: Scheduling the Interviews 20
    Step Three: Conducting the Interviews 20
    Pro Tip: Have a Conflict Management Plan 21
    Take Action 21
    Traps to Avoid 21
    Keep It Fresh 22

Chapter 4 Element: Blueprint Creation 23
    Step One: Assign Responsibility 24
    Step Two: Development Strategy 25
    Pro Tip: Plan Your MVP 25
    Take Action 25
    Traps to Avoid 26
    Keep It Fresh 26

Part 2: Foundational Elements 27
Chapter 5 Element: Discovery Questions 29
    Pro Tip: Identifying Features in the Winning Zone 29
    Step One: Features and Benefits of Your Product or Service 30

  Step Two: What Problem Would A Prospect Need to Have In Order to Care?............31
  Step Three: Developing Discovery Questions 32
  Step Four: Discovery Questions for Inbound Prospects 32
  Pro Tip: Ongoing Discovery Question Development 33
  Step Five: Adding Discovery Questions to the Playbook............................... 33
  Step Six: Questions to Uncover Resources 36
  Step Seven: Questions to Disarm Resistance 37
  Take Action 37
  Traps to Avoid.. 38
  Keep It Fresh 38

Chapter 6 Element: Personas... *39*
  Step One: Identify Your Buyer Personas... 39
  Step Two: Identify the Job-to-Be-Done for Each Buyer............................... 40
  Step Three: What Is Their Pain? 41
  Step Four: Bringing It All Together 41
  Take Action 41
  Traps to Avoid.. 42
  Keep It Fresh 42

Chapter 7 Element: The Sales Process *43*
  Tech Tip: Improve the Current Sales Process... 43
  Step One: Define the Stages 43
  Step Two: Define Exit Criteria 44
  Pro Tip: Through the Buyer's Eyes.. 45
  Take Action 45
  Traps to Avoid.. 45
  Keep It Fresh 46

Chapter 8 Element: Target Market *47*
  Step One: Identify Attributes.. 48
  Step Two: Define Target Market Segments 48
  Step Three: Lead Scoring 49
  Pro Tip: New Products or Services 50
  Take Action 50
  Traps to Avoid...51
  Keep It Fresh 51

Chapter 9 Element: Customer Stories *52*
  Pro Tip: What Is a Customer Story? 52
  Pro Tip: Capturing Customer Stories 53
  Step One: Indexing Customer Stories... 54

    Take Action 55
    Traps to Avoid 56
    Keep It Fresh 56

Chapter 10 Element: Managing Resistance (Objections) *57*
    Pro Tip: Understanding Resistance 57
    Step One: Capture Resistance Your Team Experiences 58
    Step Two: Create Examples, Categories, and Responses 59
    Take Action 60
    Traps to Avoid 60
    Keep It Fresh 61

Chapter 11 Element: Competitive Battlecards *62*
    Pro Tip: Understanding the Winning Zone 62
    Step One: Competitive Positioning 64
    Step Two: Customers Won from Competitors 64
    Take Action 65
    Traps to Avoid 65
    Keep It Fresh 65

Part 3: Account Executives (Closers) *67*
Chapter 12 Element: Product and Pricing *69*
    Step One: Product Index 70
    Step Two: Pricing Guidelines 71
    Step Three: Product Road Map 72
    Take Action 72
    Traps to Avoid 72
    Keep It Fresh 73

Chapter 13 Element: Structuring Meetings *74*
    Step One: Standardize Meeting Structures 75
    Take Action 75
    Traps to Avoid 76
    Keep It Fresh 76

Chapter 14 Element: Demos + Presentations *77*
    Step One: Preparing for the Demo 78
    Step Two: Running the Demo 78
    Pro Tip: Presentation Framework 79
    Step Three: Maintaining Velocity Post-Demo 79
    Step Four: Pull Everything Together 80
    Take Action 80

  Traps to Avoid..81
  Keep It Fresh..81

Chapter 15 Element: Create Momentum 82
  Step One: Tactics for Momentum between Meetings 82
  Step Two: Create a Cadence for Active Opportunities..................... 83
  Take Action 84
  Traps to Avoid... 84
  Keep It Fresh 84

Chapter 16 Element: Time Lines 85
  Step One: Reverse Time line to Close.................................... 85
  Step Two: Trial or Pilot Management 87
  Take Action 88
  Traps to Avoid... 88
  Keep It Fresh 88

Chapter 17 Element: Negotiation Levers 89
  Step One: Identify Negotiation Levers................................... 89
  Step Two: Create a Negotiation Balance Sheet 90
  Take Action 90
  Traps to Avoid..91
  Keep It Fresh 91

Chapter 18 Element: Content and Resources 92
  Step One: The Bray-Sorey Matrix 92
  Pro Tip: Using Microcontent.. 93
  Pro-Tip: When to Use Long-Form Content in the Sales Process 93
  Bonus Content: The Actionable Insights Map™ 94
  Take Action 99
  Traps to Avoid... 96
  Keep It Fresh 97

Chapter 19 Element: Referrals 98
  Step One: Identify Referral Opportunities 98
  Pro Tip: Ask for Referrals 99
  Pro Tip: Measure Referrals 100
  Take Action 100
  Traps to Avoid..100
  Keep It Fresh 100

Part 4: Sales Development (Prospecting and Opening Conversations) 101
Chapter 20 Element: Building a Prospect List 103
  Step One: Define the Market Segment...................................103

Step Two: Define the Persona 104
Pro Tip: Defining the Use Case 104
Step Three: Set List Goals 104
Step Four: Find Lead Information 105
Step Five: Load to CRM 105
Pro Tip: Data Hygiene 105
Pro Tip: Time Management 106
Take Action 106
Traps to Avoid 106
Keep It Fresh 106

Chapter 21 Element: Outbound Prospecting 107
Step One: Calling Framework 107
Step Two: E-mail Prospecting Templates 108
Step Three: Other Prospecting Tactics 100
Take Action 109
Traps to Avoid 109
Keep It Fresh 110

Chapter 22 Elements: Qualifying Inbound Leads 111
Step One: Identify Inbound Channels 101
Step Two: Map Inbound Channel to the Buyer's Journey 112
Step Three: Map Messaging to Inbound Activity 112
Pro Tip: Inbound E-mail Principles 113
Pro Tip: Inbound Call Principles 114
Take Action 114
Traps to Avoid 115
Keep It Fresh 115

Part 5: Additional Elements 117
Chapter 23 Element: Upsell and Cross-Sell 119
Step One: Identifying Characteristics 119
Step Two: Build a List 120
Step Three: Get a Conversation 121
Step Four: Conducting the Account Review 122
Take Action 122
Traps to Avoid 123
Keep It Fresh 123

Chapter 24 Element: Social Plays 124
Pro Tip: Social Profile Audit 124
Step One: Audience Building 125
Step Two: Audience Engagement 126
Step Three: Build Your Campaigns 127

    Take Action 127
    Traps to Avoid 128
    Keep It Fresh 128

Chapter 25 Element: Trade Shows and Conferences **129**
    Step One: Set Goals 129
    Step Two: Develop Messaging 130
    Step Three: Plan Calendars for the Event 131
    Step Four: Convert Leads to Opportunities 132
    Take Action 132
    Traps to Avoid 132
    Keep It Fresh 133

Chapter 26 Element: Playbook Glossary **134**
    Step One: Identify Key Words and Phrases 134
    Step Two: Get Agreement on Definitions 135
    Step Three: Build Competence 135
    Take Action 135
    Traps to Avoid 136
    Keep It Fresh 136

Part 6: Integrating the Playbook **137**

Chapter 27 Integration: Meeting Planning and Debriefing **139**
    Method: Personas in the Meeting 139
    Method: Relevant Use Case 140
    Method: Demo Product 141
    Method: Using Social Proof Appropriately in Meetings 141
    Method: Meeting Goals? 142
    Method: Post-Meeting Debrief 142
    Take Action 143
    Traps to Avoid 143
    Keep It Fresh 143

Chapter 28 Integration: Deployment and Continuous Improvement ... **144**
    Method: Deployment 144
    Pro Tip: When Is the Playbook "Done?" 145
    Step One: Kickoff 145
    Pro Tip: Signs the Playbook Is Succeeding or Failing 146
    Step Two: Continuous Improvement 147

Appendix A: Glossary **149**

Appendix B: Sample Interview Scripts **155**
    Executive Interview 155

Sales Rep (SDR or AE) Interview 156
For AEs Only 157

Appendix C: Other Books We've Written *159*
Triangle Selling 159
The Sales Enablement Playbook. 160
Sales Development. 162

Appendix D: Additional Resources. *165*
The ClozeLoop Engagement Model. 165

Notes. *169*

1

INTRODUCTION

A well-designed, relevant, and highly utilized sales playbook creates teams that engage with more prospects, produce more pipeline, and close more deals. A playbook creates more consistent top performers, *more quickly*. It will also close the gap between your top performers and everyone else.

Playbooks are living tools that must continue to be developed, revised, and curated over time. Growing companies are constantly hiring new people, promoting internally, entering into new markets, and facing direct or unforeseen competition. In order to drive success, an understanding of how the business operates, what has worked in the past, what is presently working, and what is anticipated to work in the future is required.

We wrote this book for CEOs and sales VPs who are anxious about their sales team's ability to scale and produce consistent results. If you're not a CEO or VP of sales, this book will still benefit you in the following roles:

Frontline Sales Manager: Equip the team with the tools they need to be effective during selling conversations and create a collaborative ecosystem where top performers can share their tips with everyone else.

Sales Enablement Leader: Build your team's first playbook or increase the effectiveness of your existing playbook by using this book as a reference guide.

Customer Success Leader: Identify and cultivate upsell and cross-sell opportunities.

Salesperson: Identify opportunities to improve performance in your current role, and position yourself for career growth.

Marketing Leader: Improve the adoption of marketing assets by the sales team and gain greater insight into those that will have a positive impact on the sales process.

Other Executive: Align finance, operations, and other functions with a more formalized infrastructure to drive repeatable growth.

Sales Consultant: Improve the quality and repeatability of your work product for clients.

Let's be honest. Building a sales playbook is not hard. Building an *effective* sales playbook is hard. Creating a culture to utilize and maintain one is even harder. We wrote this book to break down the development of a sales playbook into elements that any organization can build. If you stick with us to the end, you will be equipped with the know-how to build a comprehensive action-oriented playbook that will become a living application; not an event, a static file on your company's drive or wiki, or worse—the one-inch binder monitor stand.

What Is a Sales Playbook?

At the highest level, an individual's success in sales is a direct result of three pillars; *mindset, action,* and *skill* (fig. 1.1).

> *An effective sales playbook is the salesperson's tool for strategically planning and tactically executing the many conversations and activities required in a sales process.*

The sales playbook is a collection of actions and contexts that define an individual and organization's engagement with buyers. Think of the playbook as the sales team's collective brain, where information is stored and then accessed when sales activities occur.

Figure 1.1: The three pillars of success

The playbook is composed of *elements,* which are represented by the chapters in this book. Each element can stand alone and serves a specific function. When all the elements are combined, you have a single source of truth. This structure eliminates the need to search across different documents, folders, and databases for critical information. It's all in your playbook!

A sales playbook is not an operations manual. There are countless operational elements that are important to your business but are outside the scope of a playbook, including CRM implementation, sales technology workflow, handoffs between teams, compensation and goal alignment, team structure, company history, and so on. A sales playbook is the fuel that makes the operational engine run.

A sales playbook is also not a training manual. While strong sales playbooks augment the onboarding process and reduce the time needed to ramp up new hires, static information regarding "how to sell," how to use products in your tech stack, or even, core sales methodology that a salesperson must know in your organization are not part of a playbook. These should exist in a learning management system (LMS) or training handbook. Static documents weigh down a playbook with too much content, create a perception of being relevant only to new salespeople, and discourage daily utilization and engagement.

When to Build a Sales Playbook?

Is now the right time for your company to build a sales playbook or to refresh the one you already have? Take the ten-question quiz in figure 1.2.

Figure 1.2: Do you agree or disagree with these statements?

Statement	Disagree	Unsure	Agree
All salespeople are able to uncover pain that creates urgency.	❏	❏	❏
Salespeople tell relevant customer stories based on persona, use case, etc.	❏	❏	❏
At least 80% of deals currently have a clear next step that the prospect has agreed to.	❏	❏	❏
New hires consistently hit quota after a rapid onboarding process.	❏	❏	❏
We have as many leads as we need to hit our goals.	❏	❏	❏
90% of deals close when forecasted.	❏	❏	❏
Salespeople know how to win against each major competitor.	❏	❏	❏
Salespeople spend at least 90% of their time working on deals that close.	❏	❏	❏
Demos exclusively focus on pain that was uncovered during discovery.	❏	❏	❏
We consistently upsell and cross-sell existing customers.	❏	❏	❏

If you checked "agree" in every column, please reach out to us on LinkedIn, and we'll give you your money back for this book. You're doing great!

If you are like most people, and there is an opportunity to increase revenue, win more of the right deals, shorten sales cycles, create greater consistency, and improve individual rep performance—then you've found the right resource.

We have worked with small teams that have had go-to-market breakthroughs. We've expedited initial customer acquisition and helped identify opportunities to scale as a result of building a playbook. Larger teams who engage us do so because there is inconsistent performance across their sales team, they are often drowning in useless information overload, and they are worried about poor execution or missed opportunities.

Playbooks allow you to run sales experiments. An experiment cannot be run without a control. Standardizing operations across many playbook elements acts as that control and allows companies to run quick, impactful experiments, instead of random actions in hope of success. If you think you are in a more mature market, have figured it out, and no longer need to experiment—ask Kodak how that plan works out.

Bottom line: If you are selling or plan to sell something business-to-business, you need a playbook, and it's never too early to develop one. Wait until you've "figured it out" at your own peril.

Impact on Onboarding and Retention

According to research:

- 80% of selling conversations do not meet the expectations of executives (*Forrester*);

- 90% of marketing materials don't get used by sales personnel (*American Marketing Association*);

- 90% of sales training has no lasting impact after 120 days (*ES Research Group*).

According to Salesforce.com's *2015 State of Sales Report*, top companies are spending more than $1,000/person/year on sales training. Yet, the 2019 *State of Sales Report* shows that a full 69 percent of reps are still stuck in the "frozen middle" of moderate performance.

A sales playbook reduces onboarding time by giving a new hire much of the information he or she will need to be successful in a well-structured format. When hiring experienced salespeople, a playbook allows them to leverage their expertise and ramp up since they are familiar with all the components of the playbook in the context of the companies they have worked at before but need to be brought up to speed on the specifics for their new company faster. For example:

- They know how to leverage customer stories, but need to know your customer stories and which stories to use in which situations.

- They know how to ask discovery questions, but need to know which ones to use in various scenarios to uncover pain from prospects for your product or service.

- They know how to manage Resistance, but need to know what objections they are likely to hear and what responses are likely to work.

For experienced sales hires, combining their sales skills with the knowledge contained in your playbook gets them sales-ready, fast.

While playbooks are a critical component of new-hire onboarding, they are primarily meant to be used by ramped up salespeople on an ongoing basis. Unfortunately, many organizations equip salespeople with too little information, too late, much of which is overwhelming and poorly presented, or simply out of context. Often the focus is on product knowledge, as if just educating a buyer will result in deals closing. Salespeople need business, selling, process, and conversational tools to succeed.

Impact on Channel Partners

Companies selling their products or services through channel partners face a grueling series of challenges from partner enablement, to increasing sell-through, pipeline velocity, alignment with their goals, and quality control of the sales process.

An effective sales playbook quickly gets channel partners up to speed while providing ongoing resources on demand and quality assurance. The playbook delivered to the channel team can be the complete sales playbook, or an abbreviated version that only showcases the most relevant elements.

Triangle Selling™

We wrote the book *Triangle Selling* to underlie methodologies like Miller Heiman, MEDDIC, Challenger, and Sandler with the most comprehensive frameworks published to date. Many readers of the book choose to implement Triangle Selling as a stand-alone methodology. For those who have adopted Triangle Selling in whole or in part, we highlight the elements that correlate to these frameworks in this toolkit. **However, you need NOT be a Triangle Selling organization to use the elements in this book.**

Triangle Selling frameworks referenced in this book include the following:

- Structuring Meetings (P.L.A.N.)

- Sharing demos and customer stories (S.H.A.R.E.)

- Growing trials, pilots, and initial deals into larger engagements (G.R.O.W.)

- Helping to create urgency between meetings (H.E.L.P.)

- Measuring rapport (S.C.A.L.E.)

- Generating referrals on a systematic basis (D.O.T.S.)

Triangle Selling takes a robust view across the three critical aspects of discovery as well:

- **Reason**: Why will the prospect buy?

- **Resources**: Understand the prospect's willingness and ability to invest across seven types of Resources: emotional, intellectual, human, technical, financial, political, and energy.

- **Resistance**: In lieu of having a twenty-page "objection handling document," understand the psychology behind Resistance and how salespeople can manage it across the three types of Resistance: reactance, skepticism, and inertia.

We encourage you to tightly integrate your existing sales methodology into your playbook. However, feel free to plug in a component of Triangle Selling wherever you see fit.

How to Use This Book

This book is a builder's toolkit, not a textbook. The goal is to coach the reader along the set of actionable steps that ClozeLoop follows with each client in order to make an effective sales playbook come to life.

We wrote this book for an advanced audience. If you are new to sales, are unfamiliar with the concept of sales playbooks, or don't have thorough insight into the inner workings of each department of your organization, you will feel challenged at times. That's OK! Push yourself, engage with colleagues, and work together to build the best playbook that you can for your company.

Each chapter covers an element of the playbook. For each element, we will explore the following at the beginning of the chapter:

Goal: What is the desired outcome from employees having access to this element of the playbook?

How It's Used: Who will use this element as part of their jobs, and how? Adjust our suggestions to the structure of your organization.

Difficulty: An estimate of how difficult it will be to build out the element to the point that it can be deployed. Difficulty is defined as follows:

- **Easy**: A competent individual who understands how the sales team operates can do it by himself or herself.

- **Medium**: Collaboration within the sales team is required and might possibly involve several stakeholders.

- **Hard**: Stakeholders from multiple departments must come to agreement to complete the element.

People + Resources Required: The departments that will contribute to the creation of the element.

> *Note: We do not specifically call out "sales enablement," because we assume that if a company has a sales enablement team, they are involved in every aspect of the playbook.*

Next, we will introduce the element, steps, and relevant frameworks. We provide guidance on how to build out each framework, respecting the fact that every organization and business is different. As we introduce frameworks, we will use some example data here to demonstrate the concepts.

Most of our frameworks are built out as tables, since we find them to be the universal way to order, connect, and display information. Decide which method of displaying information works best for you.

> *Do not launch your playbook in a word-processing document or in slides. It will fail. These formats are not dynamic, make collaboration and navigation difficult, discourage a feedback loop, forestall iteration, and* **will be useless in ninety days**.

Throughout this book, we will reference TradeShowMe, a fictional company that rates trade shows by attendees, reach, value, content, and prestige. Example data inside of frameworks will guide you in applying these tools to your company.

An in-depth example playbook is available at TriangleSellingPlaybook.com.

At the end of each chapter, you'll find three sections:

> **Take Action**: Your checklist of specific next steps to make the element come to life.
>
> **Traps to Avoid**: Common mistakes we've observed over 10 years and how they can be avoided.
>
> **Keep It Fresh**: Guidelines on incorporating feedback and keeping your content up to date.

Throughout the book, if there are words, phrases, or acronyms that do not look familiar, check out the glossary in appendix A for a definition. Additionally, we have included space on each page and a few pages at the back of the book for you to take notes along the way.

Let's build your playbook!

PART 1:
PREPARING TO DEVELOP THE PLAYBOOK

2

ELEMENT: GATHERING INFORMATION

Goal: Before working on the playbook, it's smart to first gather a large amount of information that will go into it. A thorough information-gathering plan will result in a strong first version of the playbook. The key is to effectively navigate your organization to get what you need, without creating too much friction inside of your organization.

How It's Used: The playbook development team will use this element to generate the information that will be used to seed the playbook.

Difficulty: Medium

People + Resources Required:

- ❏ Sales Management ❏ Customer Success ❏ SDR Management
- ❏ Senior Execs ❏ Marketing

Step One: Specific Information You Will Need

You want to be comprehensive in the information you gather because it informs your playbook development process. Additionally, avoid sending multiple requests to the same individual, since that will make your process disorganized and burdensome. Do this work up front.

Pro Tip: Rationale for Some Assets

Board or Investor Presentations: The playbook will be successful if it directly aligns with the goals of the organization at the highest level. Some executives might be hesitant to provide access here, in which case a brief meeting to discuss the company's goals at the highest level will suffice.

Sales Presentations: Prospect decks and any other type of slide presentations that are used in selling conversations.

Org Chart: Clearly understand all the different teams, anticipated hires, and management structure. With technology that allows for the creation of dynamic playbooks, it will be possible to create tailored playbooks for specific teams and individuals.

Team and Individual Performance: Understanding how each team and individual has recently performed against goals can help inform the scope of the playbook. If there are specific areas where people need to focus to improve, ensure that these elements are addressed early. A playbook that directly contributes to organizational success will be adopted and adhered to.

Methodology: Understand the company's sales methodology. If you have several (many companies do), understand how different teams use different components of each methodology. Often you will find that the methodology(ies) in place doesn't match how the sales team actually operates day to day.

Sales Collateral: Gather the sales collateral your salespeople currently successfully use, including case studies, white papers, e-books, ROI calculators, and so on. Also try to understand specifically how these items are used *for success*. Simply sending an e-mail with a document attached and waiting to see who opens it is not proof of success.

Competitive Intel: Some organizations have strong battlecards, while others might just have a list of competitors and a few talking points. Gather what you have.

Call Recordings: Hearing your salespeople interact with prospects can identify major opportunities for the playbook. Listen to cold calls, discovery calls, demos, proposal presentations, and try to do so across the team. It will take some time, but this intel will provide direction for the playbook and can also identify WIIFM (What's in It for Me?) motivations for stakeholders, who are often shocked when they hear what salespeople are saying to prospects in the absence of a well-defined playbook.

Pipeline Review and CRM Audit: Identify problems within the pipeline and CRM hygiene (stages, fields, exit criteria, and so on) that can be positively impacted by the playbook.

Step Two: Making the Request

Our guidelines for this process include:

1. Make requests as specific as possible.

2. Offer in-person meetings, video interviews, or joint working sessions in lieu of long "homework assignments." Your colleagues are busy running their departments or performing in their roles. We have found that many people will not complete a list of requests, and if they do, they won't put in the effort that you had hoped for.

3. Have a compelling WIIFM motivation. Take every chance possible to highlight how different components of the playbook will directly or indirectly impact each stakeholder in a positive way.

4. Include a reasonable deadline.

5. Gain the endorsement of the playbook's executive sponsor if that will help drive access and urgency.

Here's an example of a request to your vice president of marketing:

Jennifer,

I am working on our sales playbook that will help

   A. the sales team to align more effectively with the marketing messages your team creates and

Notes

B. *create consistent conversions on the lead generation campaigns you are running.*

Can you help me get access to the marketing collateral we use at trade shows and links to the demo videos we are using online? You might be too busy to go digging, so I can schedule thirty minutes in a conference room to sit down next to you and cycle through what you've got if that's easier. Or, if I should be asking someone else, can you please point me in the right direction?

Alex is hoping to expedite this project, so I'd like to have access to these by next Thursday. Let me know what's best.

Step Three: Tracking Assets and Following Up

Once you have developed a list of requests and have identified who to send each request to, set a deadline to get everything back. It's wise to provide a one-week buffer since some people might be on vacation or need an extra nudge to get you what you need, but don't let this phase of the project drag on, as this work is just beginning.

Keep track of your project assets in a request table, as shown in figure 2.1.

Figure 2.1 Request table

Owner	Asset	Request Date	Received?
VP marketing	*Marketing collateral*	*September 3*	✔
	Demo videos	*September 3*	

Take Action

- ❑ Create a comprehensive list of information you want to collect.

- ❑ Identify who has the information you need and how you will ask for it. Include a compelling WIIFM motivation.

- ❑ Make sure you have a method to track what has been gathered and to follow up on requests.

Traps to Avoid

- Failure to think through all the information needed to create the playbook will cause inefficiency during playbook development and will frustrate people who are asked multiple follow-up questions over time.

- Don't urgently interrupt someone's workflow, as they have other jobs to do. Your failure to plan ahead does not constitute an emergency for them.

Notes

Notes

3

ELEMENT: INTERVIEWS

Goal: Create buy-in from stakeholders and efficiently extract information that is stored as tribal or institutional knowledge.

How It's Used: The playbook development team will use interview scripts to gather information from stakeholders across the company.

Difficulty: Easy

People + Resources Required:

❏ Playbook Development Team   ❏ Interviewees

Step One: Preparing for Interviews

Strong preparation for interviews is one of the most important parts of the playbook development process. Much of the information that will go into the playbook is currently stored in the heads of employees and will be extracted via interviews.

Prepare for the interview like a lawyer prepares for a deposition. You must:

1. Review information that has already been gathered.

2. Validate what you have learned.

3. Develop questions around apparent holes in the information.

Once you've done your analysis, identify expectations regarding what each interview will yield, including primary and secondary asks for each interview subject (fig. 3.1).

Figure 3.1: High-level interview prep

Interview Subject	Primary Asks	Secondary Asks	Validation

Pro Tip: Ensure Effective Interviews

Don't Waste People's Time. Most employees are willing to help with the playbook development process—as long as it doesn't become too much of a burden to them. Showing visible progress and including some contributions from all interviewees demonstrates that their time is respected.

Ask Open-Ended Questions. In order to get as much information as possible, ask good open-ended questions to instigate discussion. A good open-ended question typically begins with *why, how,* or *what if . . .*

Dig into Details. After asking your open-ended questions, do not be afraid to get into the weeds on details. Playbooks are not useful if filled with generalities.

Listen. Obviously, you want to pay close attention. Don't put yourself in a position to have to revisit a conversation because you missed something. Also, listen *carefully*. Even though you may have expectations of what you are going to find, respond and react to what you receive. The person being interviewed should do 80 percent to 90 percent of the talking. Playbook interviews are not the place for the interviewer to showcase his or her knowledge or opinions.

Prepare Your Questions. All interviews should start with prepared questions. Follow-up questions are expected and do not need to be prepared, but having a core script will help keep things on track and make the most of the interviews.

Step Two: Scheduling the Interviews

The first people interviewed should be those with a strong high-level understanding of the organization. Most likely, these will be executives or people in other senior roles. Later, interview people who can fill in the holes and answer open-ended questions.

If discrepancies are found when interviewing lower-level employees, circle back to the executives and figure out if there is a known resolution to the discrepancy.

Step Three: Conducting the Interviews

There are two general types of interview contexts: strategic and tactical.

An executive will provide a high-level strategy: the challenges the organization faces, opportunities that he or she sees on the horizon, and potential threats. Listen for the strategies relevant to the playbook and prepare to get the details from other folks in subsequent interviews. Executive interviews should range from sixty to ninety minutes, with the key executive sponsor providing as much time as necessary to cover all your questions in detail.

Interviews with other stakeholders should occur *after* the initial round of executive interviews. By combining your original list of questions for each stakeholder group with what was learned from the execs, you will be well positioned to uncover the information necessary to populate the first draft of the playbook. These interviews should be scheduled for thirty to sixty minutes, with company veterans or more senior folks requiring more time.

Throughout the stakeholder interviews, push them to get specific, ideally leading them to fill in gaps or help identify new information that was previously unknown. Often senior account executives (AEs), sales engineers (SEs), sales development reps (SDRs), and frontline sales managers will know of document repositories that hold gold but have been neglected.

We have included sample interview scripts in appendix B for executives, AEs, and SDRs.

Pro Tip: Have a Conflict Management Plan

When working with stakeholders across your organization, do not mistake conflicting objectives for roadblocks. Sales playbook information can cross multiple functions and departments, each with valuable insight and a different perspective. The key is to develop a plan for resolving these potential conflicts:

1. Agree on continuous improvement. Do not let perfection get in the way of results.

2. Choose the option that is most likely to impact revenue.

3. Engage the executive sponsor if the team isn't able to resolve conflict by itself.

Communicate these paths for resolution early in your interview process, and you'll likely never have to use them.

Take Action

- ❏ Identify all the people to be interviewed and create interview scripts.

- ❏ Schedule and conduct the interviews, following the tips in this element.

- ❏ Create a conflict management plan.

Traps to Avoid

1. Don't assume that interviewees should or do care about helping, even if it's logical for them to do so. They are busy. Make the interview worth their time, and stress what's in it for them whenever possible.

2. Don't go into an interview without a script.

Notes

Keep It Fresh

- After each interview, update the master interview script to include additional items that came up and should be covered in subsequent interviews, just as the playbook is updated in future iterations.

4

ELEMENT: BLUEPRINT CREATION

Goal: Reduce the time and amount of rework required to develop the playbook by building a blueprint.

How It's Used: The playbook development team will use this element to outline the blueprint of the playbook.

Difficulty: Easy

People + Resources Required:

❏ Playbook Development Team

The playbook blueprint is an outline that includes all the elements that will likely be needed in a playbook.

It's important to create a blueprint in order to:

1. Define what type of content will be gathered during playbook development

2. Begin to identify gaps

3. Begin to understand how people will use the playbook

We're often asked which element should be finished first and which can wait. The answer in almost every case is to put *something good* in each element and then iterate and expand on each one over time, with more effort placed on the elements that will have a more significant impact on the business.

Notes

Yes, we know that "do everything first" is usually not the right move in the professional world, but the goal is for the sales team to engage around a single source of truth. If salespeople still need to go other places to get information that will eventually be put in the playbook, the playbook will just add to information overload and clutter.

An example of a high-level blueprint that covers the elements that are discussed in this book is presented in figure 4.1.

Figure 4.1: The sales playbook blueprint

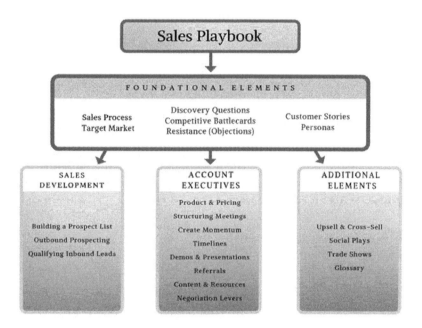

Step One: Assign Responsibility

One person should own the overall playbook project, and he or she should be in a position to hold other playbook development team members accountable to their commitments, regardless of formal reporting structure.

Each element of the playbook should be assigned to a specific person.

During the playbook development phase, it's important to track next steps and next step dates for each commitment. If people aren't meeting their commitments, the playbook owner must have the power to hold that person accountable.

To stay on track and avoid the playbook development team should meet periodically (ideally weekly) to track status and maintain momentum.

Step Two: Development Strategy

As we mentioned above, it's important to put something in each element of the playbook from the start. Worst case, spend fifteen minutes in the elements you have identified as lower priority, and plant seeds for additional information to be populated later. Interview notes are a great way to seed the playbook.

Pro Tip: Plan Your MVP

Software companies often begin their journeys by building a minimum viable product (MVP), getting it into the hands of users, receiving feedback, and iterating. Once a small group of users has validated the product, they continue to build out additional features and functionality. This way, they don't overbuild in the wrong direction. You'll do the same.

In *The Lean Startup*, author Eric Ries states (with regard to product development), "As you consider building your own minimum viable product, let this simple rule suffice: remove any feature, process, or effort that does not contribute directly to the learning you seek."

To make this concept applicable to the playbook developer, we mandate the following:

> *As you consider building your own minimum viable playbook, let this simple rule suffice: remove any element, content, or process that does not contribute directly to repeated sales team engagement, activity, and revenue impact.*

Take Action

- ❑ Create your playbook blueprint as you work through the rest of this book.
- ❑ Assign responsibility for the overall playbook, as well as each element.
- ❑ Define what is required as an MVP to launch the playbook.

Traps to Avoid

1. Failing to create a blueprint is like constructing a building without one. If you don't know where the playbook is headed at a high level, there's a good chance a lot of rework will be required, and the playbook launch date will be delayed.

2. The MVP needs to consist of useful information in each element. Additional depth can be added over time. If salespeople find elements missing in the playbook, they will continue to use other sources, and the playbook will fail to gain traction as the single source of truth for sales content.

Keep It Fresh

- Continuously update the blueprint during the playbook development process by adding and deleting elements as needed.

PART 2:
FOUNDATIONAL ELEMENTS

5

ELEMENT: DISCOVERY QUESTIONS

Goal: Develop good discovery questions that create velocity in the sales process. Standardizing discovery questions allows a sales organization to communicate consistently and to iterate quickly on the messages that have the highest impact in converting good prospects to customers and disqualifying the bad.

How It's Used:

Account Executives (AEs) and Sales Development Reps (SDRs): Identify new business opportunities.

Sales Management: Ensure that salespeople are asking pain-based discovery questions instead of talking about product features.

Customer Success Managers (CSMs): Identify upsell and cross-sell opportunities.

Difficulty: Medium

People + Resources Required:

❏ Tenured Sales Reps   ❏ Sales Management   ❏ SDR Management

Pro Tip: Identifying Features in the Winning Zone

The best salespeople ask pain-based discovery questions about topics that are relevant to their prospect persona and fit into the salesperson's winning zone. The winning zone (fig. 5.1) is the specific area where your company wins against the competition.

Figure 5.1: The winning zone

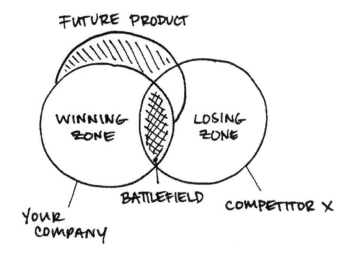

If the salesperson is able to uncover buyer pain in the winning zone, he or she is in a good position to win the deal. If not, there's still an opportunity to find pain in the battlefield or in the future winning zone, which will exist after the expansion of the current product or service offering. The last two options will result in a longer and more challenging sales process, but sales management might feel that these conversations are still worthwhile.

Salespeople who have conversations in the losing zone, where the competition has a clear advantage, are simply wasting their time.

Defining where each discovery question fits into figure 5.1 is a key component of the playbook.

Step One: Features and Benefits of Your Product or Service

Use figure 5.2 to make an exhaustive list of all your products' or services' key features. For each feature, list three to five benefits. If the list of features is extensive, focus only on those that clearly fall into your winning zone.

A feature is defined as a specific attribute of a product or service, while a benefit describes the positive outcome or result of using that feature.

> *For example, a feature of this book is clear tables for data, and a benefit of tables is that you can focus on collecting the data and not worry about frameworks for organizing them.*

Figure 5.2: Define the features and benefits for your product or service

Feature	Benefit

Step Two: What Problem Would A Prospect Need to Have In Order to Care?

Is each problem significant enough to inspire action? It will be tempting to add things like "cost" and "inefficiency" as problems, but avoid these responses. They are symptoms of something deeper, which is where the real problem lies.

Complete column C of figure 5.3 by answering the question "What problem would a prospect need to have today in order to care about this specific benefit?" These should be statements.

Figure 5.3: Aligning benefits to prospect problems

A	B	C
Feature	Benefit	Problem

We like to refer to the "feature > benefit > problem statement" framework as the *Pain Finder*.

Step Three: Developing Discovery Questions

Once you are satisfied that the problem statements are well defined, it's time to develop discovery questions.

> In Triangle Selling, we incorporate three components when building discovery questions:
>
> 1. **Problem Statement**: Include the problem statement from the previous section.
>
> 2. **CAUSE**: This acronym refers to the emotional words *concerned, anxious, upset, struggling,* and *exhausted*. Inserting emotional words in a discovery question helps appeal to the prospect's limbic (emotional) brain and helps discover pain.
>
> 3. **Social Proof**: Introducing social proof creates likeness with the prospect and builds credibility for the salesperson.
>
> The framework of the discovery question is as follows:
>
> *We're working with [Persona]s (social proof) who are struggling with (CAUSE) [Insert Problem Statement]. Does that resonate with you? (question)*

Step Four: Discovery Questions for Inbound Prospects

Inbound sales development teams work with prospects that have signaled interest in their company. The "interest" shown might be as simple as filling out a form on the company's website, or prospects might have used the product or service in a prior company. To ensure that a salesperson is able to maintain control of the conversation, we incorporate these inquiries into the discovery questions.

By adding column A in figure 5.4, it's easy to align the discovery with the inquiry instead of pitching.

Figure 5.4: Developing problem statements based on inbound inquiries

A	B	C	D
Inquiry	Relevant Feature	Benefit	Problem

Populate column A with all of the phrases that prospects use when describing why they reached out to your company.

Pro Tip: Ongoing Discovery Question Development

Discovery question development should be a part of every new product release. The ability to create pain-oriented discovery questions using the framework outlined in this chapter adds a critical component to the product release cycle that will have a substantial impact on the sales team's ability to position conversations in the winning zone and realize revenue based upon product evolution.

In addition to your typical product or service release agenda, these meetings must:

1. Demonstrate new features

2. Explain the benefits of each feature

3. Explain competitive advantages now realized

4. Develop discovery questions based upon the new feature set

Step Five: Adding Discovery Questions to the Playbook

Depending upon your business, there are three different ways to present discovery questions to users.

Notes

The first method is outlined in figure 5.5, where we segment discovery questions by persona.

Figure 5.5: Segmenting discovery questions by persona

Persona	Discovery Question
VP marketing	
VP sales	

Use this view if *persona* is the main driver of discovery.

Another option is shown in figure 5.6, where the questions are segmented by use case.

Figure 5.6: Segmenting discovery questions by use case

Use Case	Discovery Question
Use case 1	
Use case 2	

Use this method if the *use case is relevant to many personas*, and discovery questions will not change from persona to persona.

The third approach is shown in figure 5.7, where discovery questions relate to both a persona and a use case.

Figure 5.7: Segmenting discovery questions by persona and use case

A	B	C
Use Case	**Persona**	**Discovery Question**
Use case 1	VP marketing	
	VP sales	
Use case 2	VP marketing	
	Director of field marketing	

Use this method if *different personas are going to care about different use cases for different reasons.*

In most situations, asking one discovery question will lead to logical follow-ups (fig. 5.8).

Figure 5.8: Logical follow-up questions

A	B	C
Persona	**Discovery Question**	**Logical Follow-Up**
VP marketing		
VP sales		

Do not become overly controlling and develop full conversation scripts here. They won't be useful. But, if there are specific follow-up questions that should be asked, note them here to assist the salesperson.

> In Triangle Selling, insert the Priority Path framework, which includes six sequential questions, ending with the prospect stating where solving the pain falls on his or her priority list.
>
> For many discovery questions, the Priority Path is the logical follow-up, but depending upon your business, other specific questions might make sense as an intermediate step.

Step Six: Questions to Uncover Resources

A critical part of discovery is the ability of the salesperson to uncover the Resources that a prospect is willing and able to sacrifice to resolve their pain or realize an opportunity (fig. 5.9).

Figure 5.9: Questions to uncover Resources

A	B	C
Resource	**Prospect Says**	**Discovery Question**
Intellectual		
Emotional		
Technology		
Human		
Financial		
Political		
Battery		

Determine the types of Resources you want your salespeople to uncover, and develop questions help them do so. Completed tables can be found at TriangleSellingPlaybook.com.

Step Seven: Questions to Disarm Resistance

It's essential to shed light on Resistance in discovery (fig. 5.10). Unspoken Resistance will leave a salesperson expending energy on the wrong deals.

Figure 5.10: Questions to disarm Resistance

A	B	C
Resistance	**Prospect Says**	**Discovery Question**
Reactance		
Skepticism		
Inertia		

Your sales methodology may advocate objection handling as part of the selling process. If so use the framework in figure 5.11.

Figure 5.11: General objection handling framework

Objection	Validation	Response

Take Action

- ❏ Complete a Pain Finder (feature > benefit > problem statement) table for each key feature of your company's product or service. There should be at least two to three benefits and problem statements for each feature.

- ❏ Create a bank of pain-focused discovery questions, using a combination of problem statements, social proof, and CAUSE.

- ❏ Develop questions to uncover Resources and Resistance.

Traps to Avoid

1. Asking questions that do not fit into your winning zone will lead to long sales cycles or lost deals.

2. While most organizations will find their sales team having conversations specific to five to seven discovery questions, it's important to be exhaustive in this exercise so that salespeople are able to maximize all opportunities in the winning zone—not just those that are common.

Keep It Fresh

- For each new product feature that is released, complete the Pain Finder to develop new discovery questions.

- As sales managers listen to and coach calls, they should update this list with new discovery questions that are effective and remove those that are obsolete.

6

ELEMENT: PERSONAS

Goal: By knowing their buyer personas inside and out, salespeople are better able to establish and maintain rapport, move more quickly toward becoming a trusted advisor, uncover pain, and create velocity in the sales process.

How It's Used:

Marketing Team: Relevant messaging is more likely to inspire prospect activity.

SDRs: Maximize the number of meetings scheduled for AEs by using messaging relevant to each persona.

AEs: Discovery questions, product demos, customer stories, and all other forms of communication should be relevant to the prospect's persona in order to uncover pain, build rapport, and overcome Resistance.

Difficulty: Hard

People + Resources Required:

- ❏ Sales Management
- ❏ Customer Success
- ❏ Marketing

Step One: Identify Your Buyer Personas

First, group similar prospect job titles into buyer personas. For example, if your target executive is the VP of marketing, this persona will

Notes

also include people with the titles head of marketing and chief marketing officer. If there is no material difference in how you would market to two different job titles, group them together into a single persona.

Start by identifying your top three buyer personas. You can add more later.

1. _____

2. _____

3. _____

Step Two: Identify the Job-to-Be-Done for Each Buyer

Clayton Christensen, in his book *The Innovator's Solution*, talks about the concept of a "job-to-be-done" (JTBD). Most organizations are selling to roles or titles in an organization with very little understanding of what those individuals are tasked with accomplishing, who is holding them accountable, the resources they have available, and how they go about doing their job.

Complete figure 6.1 for each of your target personas.

Figure 6.1: Understanding buyer personas

Persona	Reports To	Goals	Manages	Workflow
VP of marketing	*CEO*	• *ID and reach target customers (online, print, and trade shows)* • *Increase inbound lead volume*	• *Internal marketing department* • *External vendors like PR firm*	• *Buy ads* • *Sponsor trade shows* • *Develop messages* • *Evaluate campaigns*

From your complete table, your salesperson can now explain the following:

> *We work with VPs of Marketing who report to the CEO. Their goals are often to increase inbound lead volume by identifying where their target customers are and reaching them with relevant messages online, in print, and through trade shows. They purchase advertising, sponsor trade shows, develop and design messages, and evaluate campaigns with a team that can include an external PR firm and the internal marketing team.*

Step Three: What Is Their Pain?

Effective sales conversations create urgency and commitment by uncovering the buyer's pain (fig. 6.2). Pain-based conversations disqualify quickly as well.

Figure 6.2: Tie pain your product solves to the relevant persona

Feature	Benefit	Pain	Relevant Persona

You have just created a competitive advantage! While your competition is running around town talking at people regarding features and benefits, you can now say:

> *We work with VPs of marketing who are struggling to measure the return on investment of event sponsorship.*

Step Four: Bringing It All Together

Your playbook should make it easy for a salesperson to readily reference the persona element's highlights in one view (fig. 6.3).

Figure 6.3: Persona elements in one view.

Persona	Workflow	Their Pain	How We Win

Take Action

- ❑ Define your buyer personas.
- ❑ Complete figure 6.1 to describe each persona's relevant attributes.
- ❑ Identify the pain each persona has that your product or service can solve.
- ❑ Identify specifically how your company wins with each persona.

Traps to Avoid

1. If your salespeople don't understand what your buyers do, they will have a hard time having peer based business conversations with them.

2. Make sure that the pain identified is specifically relevant to the buyer persona. Administrative issues are less likely to be relevant to executives, and high-level strategy isn't relevant to nonexecutive employees.

3. Ensure that pain identified is real pain. Things like "inefficiency" and "high cost" are not pain; they might be symptoms of pain.

Keep It Fresh

- Conduct an in-depth audit on a quarterly basis. Specifically, ask the following questions:

    o Are we targeting any new personas?

    o Has anything changed in the JTBD of our target personas?

    o Has "how we win" changed?

- Update whenever a new feature is released.

7

ELEMENT: THE SALES PROCESS

Goal: A strong sales process allows the sales team to close deals rapidly and predictably.

How It's Used: All employees involved in the sales process (or on either end of it) must understand what's happening before them, what their role is, and what happens after their contribution is made.

Difficulty: Medium

People + Resources Required:

- ❑ Sales Team
- ❑ Sales Leadership
- ❑ Sales Engineering
- ❑ Other Sales Functions

Tech Tip: Improve the Current Sales Process

Your company probably already has a sales process defined and rolled out through the CRM, but if there are opportunities to improve the current state, the rollout of a sales playbook can be a great catalyst.

Step One: Define the Stages

The sales process should include a series of stages, where each stage either disqualifies or takes the prospect one step further toward becoming a customer.

In certain cases, the easiest way to shorten a sales cycle is to actually *add a stage*. Sometimes sales stages are designed to expedite the sale without taking into account that a buyer has to have had a reasonable amount and quality (uncovered problems or pain) of engagement with the salesperson to confidently take a next step.

Sales stages should be linear, and each additional stage should represent demonstrable progress toward a signed contract (fig. 7.1). Events that can happen in out of chronology or only in certain circumstances should not be stages, but rather non-stage fields in the CRM.

Figure 7.1: Sales stages

Sales Stage
1 - *Qualification*
2 - *Demo*
3 - *Proposal*
4 - *Closing*
5 - *Won*

Step Two: Define Exit Criteria

Now that you have defined each stage, it's time to add exit criteria (fig. 7.2). These are the mandatory or recommended guidelines to be achieved in order to move an opportunity to the next stage.

Figure 7.2: Exit criteria for each sales stage

Sales Stage	Exit Criteria
1 - *Qualification*	
2 - *Demo*	
3 - *Proposal*	
4 - *Closing*	
5 - *Won*	

Exit criteria must be specific and clear. Anyone looking at a deal in the CRM should be able to tell if required exit criteria have been met.

Pro Tip: Through the Buyer's Eyes

In addition to defining what happens within your sales team and CRM, you need to understand your buyer's journey, and how it aligns with your sales process (fig. 7.3).

Figure 7.3: Mapping the sales process to the buyer's journey

Sales Team	Qualify	Demo	Proposal	Close
Prospect	Disclose selective information	Gather information	Think it over	Negotiate

Initially, you might not be clear on what the buyer's journey involves. Your existing customers are a great resource for learning this information. Companies also often distinguish the buyer's journey based upon company size, industry vertical, and so on.

Take Action

- ❏ Document each stage in the sales process.

- ❏ Define exit criteria for each stage. Different criteria may exist for different market segments (enterprise vs. small business) or other prospect attributes, such as the product being sold.

- ❏ Objectively describe what is happening from the buyer's perspective at each stage of the sales process.

Traps to Avoid

1. Creating too many stages will create confusion, which will in turn decrease forecast accuracy.

2. Not having enough stages slows velocity. Each stage must either disqualify or be like fuel. Not enough fuel, and the engine sputters out. That's how deals stall.

Notes

3. Once the sales process is published, avoid letting salespeople move deals without satisfying exit criteria. If you find yourself inclined to do so, reevaluate the exit criteria and adjust accordingly.

Keep It Fresh

- Review the sales process on a quarterly basis.

- Review the relevance of exit criteria quarterly and make adjustments as needed. The goal is to create velocity, not administrative work.

8

ELEMENT: TARGET MARKET

Goal: Focusing on a defined target market ensures that sales resources are deployed where they will result in consistent wins.

How It's Used:

Marketing and SDRs: Determine where to focus marketing and prospecting energy.

AEs: Prioritize energy during the sales process.

CSMs: As CSMs see how the product or service is used in the wild, suggest adjustments to the target market.

Difficulty: Hard

People + Resources Required:

- ❏ Sales Leadership
- ❏ Marketing
- ❏ Customer Success
- ❏ Other Internal Experts

Notes

Step One: Identify Attributes

Identify basic criteria to determine the quality of a prospect.

Typical attributes include the following:

Company Size	**Geography**	**Industry**
Event	**Job Title**	**Incumbent Solution**
Number of Employees	**Language**	**Technology**

Get started by listing at least five attributes, keeping in mind that more can be added over time.

1. _____
2. _____
3. _____
4. _____
5. _____
6. _____
7. _____

Step Two: Define Target Market Segments

Now that you have some attributes, the next step is to create a table like the one shown in figure 8.1. This diagram shows the specific values of each attribute that make a prospect ideal, good, or rejected.

Figure 8.1: The target market

Attribute	Ideal	Good	Rejected
Company size			
Geography			
Current solution			

Get values into each of these cells. Sometimes adjacent columns might have the same value, and that's fine.

If your company sells multiple products in different target markets, you will eventually want to replicate this diagram for each product, or develop a more robust framework that includes them all.

Step Three: Lead Scoring

Combinations of attributes determine whether or not a prospect is a target. The lead score is the formula that identifies how well these attributes align with your target market. In a scoring model, each attribute will have a weight, and each prospect company will be scored based on their aggregate attributes.

Figure 8.2 is an example of a formula to determine if a lead is worth pursuing.

> In this example *attribute weight* indicates how important attributes such as company size and geography are to this company.
>
> The formula to score a lead in this example is:
>
> Score = (5 * [Company Size]) + (2 * [Geography])
>
> For example: A prospect has 150 employees and is located in the United Kingdom.
>
> 1. Figure out if these values are ideal, good, or rejected from figure 8.1.
>
> 2. Look up their respective values in figure 8.2 The resulting formula in this scenario would be:
>
> Score = (5 * 10) + (2 * 2)

Notes

As a result, the score is 54. Once all leads are scored, they can be stack ranked and prioritized. With a large volume of leads, this process is usually wired into the CRM. The logic must exist in your playbook.

Figure 8.2: Lead scoring

Attribute	Attribute Weight	Rejected	Good	Ideal
Company size	5	–100	4	10
Geography	2	–100	2	7
Current solution	3	–100	5	8

Pro Tip: New Products or Services

As new products or services are developed, define how they fit into the target market before the sales team begins selling. When defining or confirming the target market, you must:

1. Spin up a tiger team of stakeholders from product, marketing, sales development, sales, customer success, and other relevant departments;

2. Reflect on prior conversations with prospects and customers to develop a hypothetical target market for the new product or service;

3. Assign tasks to each member of the tiger team to test the hypothesis;

4. Iterate as necessary.

If your company consistently develops products or services, expect your target market to evolve. Replicate figure 8.1 to show the relevant future target market(s) so that your team will have an idea where the company is headed.

Take Action

❑ Define the key attributes for your target market.

❑ Define the target market segments, as shown in figure 8.1.

❏ Decide if lead scoring is going to be part of your playbook.

Traps to Avoid

1. Failing to think through all of the attributes of the target market and the values of each will result in a lack of focus across the sales team.

2. A company without a well-defined target market is at risk of not aligning sales activities with those of other departments.

Keep It Fresh

- Review won and lost deals on a quarterly basis and adjust the target market based on insights. If your company seems to always win or lose deals in different market segments, ensure that this information is reflected in the target market element of the playbook.

- Analyze the profitability of each market segment and make adjustments based upon your findings.

Notes

9

ELEMENT: CUSTOMER STORIES

Goal: Reduce prospect skepticism and create trust by telling stories of how you've worked with a similar persona who was experiencing a similar problem.

How It's Used:

SDRs and AEs: Build rapport by demonstrating that others similar to the prospect have found success with the product or service in the past.

CSMs: Develop new upsell and cross-sell opportunities.

Difficulty: Medium-Hard

People + Resources Required:

- ❏ Tenured Sales Reps
- ❏ Customer Success
- ❏ Marketing
- ❏ Senior Management

Pro Tip: What Is a Customer Story?

There is sometimes confusion around what constitutes a customer story. Stories come in various shapes and sizes and can range from a formal legal department-approved case study, all the way down to a quick sentence quoting a customer. Here are a couple of examples for TradeShowMe:

Last week a customer told us that they increased revenue from trade shows 3x in the last year, with no additional spending.

One prospect I worked with had not even heard of what are now their three most profitable trade shows until they got access to our dashboards.

A VP of marketing at one of our Fortune 1000 clients said that they have cut trade show budget by 23 percent while increasing trade show associated revenue by 33 percent.

Pro Tip: Capturing Customer Stories

While many salespeople think that their companies don't have enough case studies, there are often an abundance of customer stories floating around an organization, though they might not be documented. Customer stories can be farmed from the following groups within a company:

> **Customer success or account management** teams, who are interacting with customers on a daily basis. Understanding the success that these people have had with the product and feeding this information back to the sales team is an incredibly valuable exercise. It's not necessary to funnel all stories through marketing and legal to create a formal case study, but instead, a simple closed-loop communication system between customer success and sales can ensure that a relevant story exists for most selling situations.
>
> **Sales and sales engineering** teams have access to what "will work" for prospects, and even though implementation isn't complete, they can still contribute stories related to why people initially engaged in a discussion with their company.
>
> **Implementation** teams might have the most detailed knowledge related to how the new solution is different from the old, as they will dig deeper than both sales and customer success teams into the customer's business. Depending on your organization, you might not have an implementation team, and if you do, it might be internal, or operate externally through a partner.

Notes

Sales development, customer support, and sales teams can also provide a number of stories related to why a prospect chose not to buy or renew. Listening to these stories and aligning them with the future product road map and strategy can unlock insights that might not be visible otherwise. Just because you lost a deal or a customer this year doesn't mean that you won't be able to help them in the future.

It is key that customer stories are concise, specific, and accurate. If salespeople have the ability to easily find a story for any selling situation, they can then deliver it to the prospect using a storytelling framework, like S.H.A.R.E. in Triangle Selling.

> *Triangle Selling Framework*: S.H.A.R.E.
>
> *The acronym to remember what's important in a customer story, presentation, or demo.*
>
> **Simple**: *The best demos are simple and easy to understand.*
>
> **Highlight**: *To create a captivating and persuasive story line, it's critical to be compelling from the very start of the meeting.*
>
> **Acute**: *Salespeople must demonstrate their keen understanding of a prospect's pain and focus the solution on the acute reason a prospect would buy.*
>
> **Relevant**: *It is essential that the presentation is relevant to the problem, the person, and the organization.*
>
> **Engaging**: *The goal is to more deeply engage prospects in conversation, which will allow them to determine if they want to move from their comfort zone to action.*

Customer stories are a key type of microcontent that is discussed further in chapter 18.

Step One: Indexing Customer Stories

Start by developing a matrix that outlines the customer stories you need. This way, you can track progress and keep an eye on stories that remain to be captured.

Figure 9.1 shows a basic matrix where customer stories are captured by persona.

Figure 9.1 Stories by persona

Persona	Customer	Pain	Solution	Results
VP marketing	Acme Co.	Can't justify spending in terms of leads, reach, and partnering	Subscribed to TradeShowMe analysis tool for one year	Reduced their trade show budget by 23% with 33% more revenue impact

In cases where stories would be different for each persona depending on their industry, use a layout like that in figure 9.2.

Use this table if

- Personas in different industries use your product in different ways

- Applying industry context is necessary for the story to resonate with prospects

Figure 9.2: Stories by persona and industry

Persona	Industry 1				Industry 2			
	Customer	Pain	Solution	Results	Customer	Pain	Solution	Results
Persona A								
Persona B								
Persona C								

We've worked with clients who substitute "use case" for "industry." The goal is not to cover every edge case, but rather to provide salespeople with easy-to-find and easy-to-articulate stories relevant to their most common selling conversations. The fewer the words, the more likely they are able to quickly find what they need and put it to use.

Take Action

- ❏ Create a plan to capture customer stories and then execute.

- ❏ Index the customer stories in a way that makes them easy to find.

❑ Develop a plan to capture more stories on an ongoing basis.

❑ Create a specific goal for how many new customer stories will be developed each quarter in the future.

Traps to Avoid

1. Sometimes the people who have direct relationships with customers push back on the development of customer stories. Hear their concerns, demonstrate the value to the organization around why stories are important to drive revenue, and engage an executive sponsor if conflict persists.

2. Ensure that customer stories tie to specific and accurate ways that customers used your product or service to reduce pain or unlock reward. Avoid fluff at all cost.

Keep It Fresh

- Create a culture of cultivating customer stories and adding them to the playbook.

- Audit customer stories on a quarterly basis and identify gaps that need to be filled.

10

ELEMENT: MANAGING RESISTANCE (OBJECTIONS)

Goal: Salespeople who effectively manage Resistance increase the probability of winning deals the right deals and disqualify losers more quickly.

How It's Used: AEs, SDRs, and CSMs will use these tactics when running into Resistance from prospects.

Difficulty: Medium

People + Resources Required:

❏ Sales Management ❏ Tenured Sales Reps ❏ Customer Success

❏ SDR Management ❏ Tenured SDRs

Pro Tip: Understanding Resistance

Throughout the sales process, prospects will introduce various forms of Resistance.

In our sample playbook at TriangleSellingPlaybook.com, we provide tactics to categorize and respond to each of these types of Resistance.

Step One: Capture Resistance Your Team Experiences

Your organization might already have documents that list common objections. If so, much of your work is done. Otherwise, the knowledge is tribal and exists largely in the heads of salespeople and frontline managers.

Write out the top ten objections your team hears. Do not include responses yet.

1. _____

2. _____

3. _____

4. _____

5. _____

6. _____

7. _____

8. _____

9. _____

10. _____

To a salesperson, Resistance often looks like one of the following:

No money
No urgency
No problem
No trust
No confidence in successful outcome

In his book, *Resistance & Persuasion*, Dr. Eric Knowles distilled Resistance down to three common themes:

Reactance
Skepticism
Inertia

In Triangle Selling, we focus on the themes defined by Dr. Knowles, which make clear that Resistance is a natural human behavior, not an impediment to the sales cycle.

> *Triangle Selling Framework*: Resistance
>
> **Reactance** is resistance to the sales process itself. It's that stubborn kid in all of us who says, "I will not be sold!," "I don't have to do this!," "I know what you're up to, Salesperson!"
>
> **Skepticism** is Resistance against the offer. It appears when the buyer doesn't think a vendor's offering works, won't work for them, or won't work for them right now.
>
> **Inertia** is the biggest challenge a salesperson will face. Self-preservation has paralyzed the prospect. This person does nothing, possibly because past failures and disappointments are replaying over and over in his or her mind. Or they might believe that they already own or understand what they're being sold. Status and the perception of the current state being "just fine" are what's at work here.
>
> Tactics for managing Resistance include:
>
> > **Reactance**: use stories, minimize requests, use "yes and . . ." to elaborate, validate, and disqualify;
> >
> > **Skepticism**: create a guarantee, reframe the offer, reframe the resistance, and focus on the future;
> >
> > **Inertia**: disrupt and reframe the Resistance, acknowledge inertia, reciprocity, and "do the math" by quantifying the consequences of doing nothing.

Step Two: Create Examples, Categories, and Responses

The goal of this framework is not for salespeople to memorize responses but to have a single source of truth for the Resistance an organization has experienced so that these interactions will not be unfamiliar when encountered (fig. 10.1).

Notes

The salesperson must be able to:

1. Identify Resistance

2. Apply a technique (question or active listening)

3. Think of what to do next, while listening to the prospect continue to talk, which is ideally another question or a statement with a question tagged onto the end

Figure 10.1: The index of previously heard Resistance

A	B	C	D
Example	Type (Reactance, Skepticism, or Inertia)	Technique	Response
I don't think your product solves our problem.	*Skepticism*	*Validate and then ask a clarifying question.*	*That might be the case. Can you help me understand the areas our product misses the mark?*

Take Action

❑ Capture common Resistance your team hears.

❑ Develop responses that are most likely to work when the Resistance is heard.

Traps to Avoid

1. Defensive or dismissive statements often amplify Resistance, along with trying to convince prospects by positioning features and benefits.

2. Ensure that the team understands good responses *and* the underlying techniques as well.

Keep It Fresh

- Encourage all customer-facing employees to suggest additions to the playbook as they face new Resistance and find new tactics that work to manage it.

- Managers must update existing tactics to manage Resistance based upon observations of successful (quick disqualification or conversion) outcomes of real conversations.

Notes

11

ELEMENT: COMPETITIVE BATTLECARDS

Goal: Objectively knowing where a company wins, loses, and battles allows for a salesperson to understand where to focus a conversation and where to commit selling resources.

How It's Used:

AEs, SDRs, and CSMs: Effectively discuss the competition with prospects and customers.

AEs and CSMs: Position proposals for new business, upsells, and cross-sells in a way that is most likely to win against the competition.

Difficulty: Hard

People + Resources Required:

- ❑ Sales Management
- ❑ Marketing
- ❑ Customer Success
- ❑ Tenured Sales Reps

Pro Tip: Understanding the Winning Zone

Salespeople must understand the specific scenarios where they are uniquely positioned to win against the competition. Figure 11.1 was first introduced in chapter 5. Here, it outlines the competitive landscape using the winning zone framework.

Figure 11.1: The winning zone

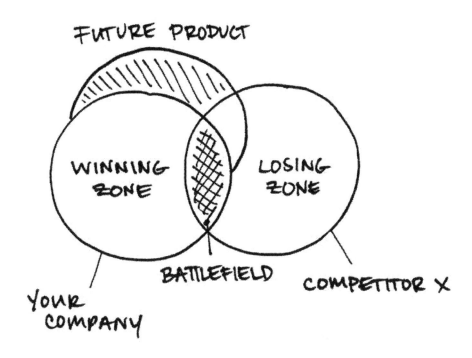

Companies develop features with the hope that those features will benefit specific personas who are experiencing problems, and that the potential resolution of the problems will compel them to make a purchase (chapter 5, discovery questions).

In a competitive marketplace, there may be overlap in these features: some in which a competitor's feature is even better (or better for a specific use case, industry, or persona) than yours. We call this the *losing zone*. We lose deals to our competitors when the pain uncovered best lends itself to these features.

Others' features may have parity. This is where our solution and a competitor's solution are very much alike. Conversations here often commoditize a product offering and create a race to the bottom price.

Ideally, you want to have conversations which fall into your winning zone. This is the area in which your feature stands alone either as unique or best-in-class. When conversations are focused here, you optimize your chance to win deals.

To remain competitive, future products are always being developed in hopes of expanding your winning zone.

Step One: Competitive Positioning

The traditional method of presenting a competitive landscape is outlined in figure 11.2, where the facts are outlined in a table.

Figure 11.2: Traditional competitive landscape

Competitor	Win	Battle	Lose

Does your organization compete against a large number of companies? Each with similar business models and competitive attributes? For example, TradeShowMe competes with hundreds of different types of marketing products and consulting firms that can be grouped into categories for competitive analysis. In this case, we'll create competitor-specific battlecards for the most common competitors (fig. 11.2) and group the rest of the competitive market, as shown in figure 11.3.

Figure 11.3: Competitive category battlecard

Competitor Category	Win	Battle	Lose
Trade show consulting firms	*Less expensive, real-time data, broader view, 24/7 access*	*Robust calculations, industry expertise*	*Customized to specific company, budget recommendations, industry discounts*
Trade show analytics products			
Internal field marketing teams			

Step Two: Customers Won from Competitors

One of the most effective ways to talk about the competition is to tell stories about customers that switched from a competitor to your product or service (fig. 11.4).

Figure 11.4: Customers won from competitors

Competitor	Customer	Reason They Switched
Competitor A		
Competitor B		

Take Action

- ☐ Identify your company's winning zone, losing zone, and battlefield.

- ☐ Develop competitive battlecards for each major competitor. If there are more than ten competitors, and each can be broken down into a handful of categories, do that as well.

- ☐ Create a list of customers that switched from competitors to your product or service.

Traps to Avoid

1. Ensure that the winning zone is objective and does not irrationally favor your company. The way to test this question is to ask, "If a salesperson left your company tomorrow and began working for your competitor, would that person still believe what is written on the battlecard to be true?" If not, adjust it.

2. The typical battlecard outlines a company's strengths and weaknesses against each of its competitors, with the bias of "we're better than them." Modern buyers have little to no information gate and can find out a ton of information about product or service without ever engaging a salesperson, so battlecards must be objective.

Keep It Fresh

- Conduct quarterly competitive audits that include qualitative feedback from the sales team, as well as quantitative analysis of deals that were won and lost.

- Ensure that everyone talking with customers and prospects adds competitive intel as it is learned.

- As customers leave the competition in favor of your company, add this intel to figure 11.4.

PART 3:
ACCOUNT EXECUTIVES (CLOSERS)

12

ELEMENT: PRODUCT AND PRICING

Note: For simplicity, we will refer to all products and services as "products" in this chapter. If your company sells a service, the same principles apply.

Goal: Clear product definitions and pricing guidelines force salespeople to maintain margins and avoid using discounting as a lever to close deals.

How It's Used: AEs will determine which product(s) are appropriate for each prospect and what price to quote.

Difficulty: Hard

People + Resources Required:

- ❏ Sales Leadership
- ❏ Product Marketing
- ❏ Executives

The products element of your playbook should be intentionally limited. The reason is simple:

> *Prospects don't care about a vendor's product. They care about resolving their pain or realizing a reward.*

In this chapter, we will focus on your products, their pricing, and your product road map. When a buyer asks your salespeople, "What does your company do?" they can either respond, "We sell trade show software" or "We work with marketing leaders who were struggling to hit their lead quotas and are frustrated with their recent outcome of trade shows they have sponsored." Which do you think will be more compelling to a buyer?

That's why we focus less on the products element of the playbook than some people might.

Step One: Product Index

If your company sells multiple products, or bundles products in different ways, you need to create a product index, like figure 12.1.

Figure 12.1: Pain-focused product index by persona

Product	Pain Solved	Persona Who Cares
Trade show analytics data	Inability to hit lead goals at trade shows	VP marketing

If your product's success depends more on market segment than persona, then replace "persona who cares" with "market segment that cares" as in figure 12.2.

Figure 12.2: Pain-focused product index by market segment

Product	Pain Solved	Market Segment That Cares
Trade show analytics data	Inability to hit lead goals at trade shows	Companies that present at trade shows

If persona and market segment both matter, then add an additional column for market segment (fig. 12.3).

Figure 12.3: Pain-focused product index by persona and market segment

Product	Pain Solved	Persona Who Cares	Market Segment That Cares
Trade show analytics data	Inability to hit lead goals at trade shows	VP marketing	Companies that present at trade shows

Step Two: Pricing Guidelines

Modern buyers expect transparent pricing early in the sales process. Furthermore, salespeople who are able to discuss pricing early and are often able to quickly disqualify prospects who are unwilling or unable to buy your product or service.

There are many ways to price a product. Figure 12.4 shows the product-based approach.

Figure 12.4: Product-based (or package-based) pricing guidelines

Product or Package	Pricing

Use this method if stand-alone products or services are being sold. Figure 12.5 shows a user-based approach.

Figure 12.5: User-based pricing guidelines

Users	Price Per User
<25	
26–100	
101–500	
500+	

This model is relevant for some types of software products, as well as different types of professional services offerings.

For organizations with more complex product offerings and pricing options, explore some additional ways to think about pricing at TriangleSellingPlaybook.com. All pricing guidelines should be easy to navigate and clear to the salesperson.

Step Three: Product Road Map

Salespeople must understand the near-term product road map and how to talk about it with prospects (fig. 12.6). In some cases, it might make sense for them to be also involved in longer-term product vision if they have a large sales cycle or other factors are in place. Keep in mind that the "What Problem It Solves" should not be a problem that exists with your own product or service. This again is a problem your prospect is experiencing.

Figure 12.6: The product road map

Timing	Feature	Benefit	What Problem It Solves
Q1 20XX			
Q2 20XX			

Take Action

❏ Document the products being sold and the pain that they solve for different personas. Add an additional filter for market segment, if applicable.

❏ Document your pricing guidelines for each product.

❏ Document the product road map and ensure there is a process to keep it fresh.

Traps to Avoid

1. Ensure that salespeople are trained to talk about the problems their prospects have, not the products their company makes.

2. Failure to have clear pricing guidelines creates distrust in prospects and ambiguity for salespeople.

Keep It Fresh

- Update each time a new product is released.

- Audit quarterly based on qualitative data from AEs and CSMs, as well as quantitative analysis of deals that were won and lost.

Notes

13

ELEMENT: STRUCTURING MEETINGS

Goal: Keep meetings on track and create velocity from meeting to meeting, until a deal is signed or the prospect is disqualified.

How It's Used:

AEs and SDRs: Structure meetings and maintain velocity during the sales process.

CSMs: Keep velocity post-sale to drive toward upsell, cross-sell, and renewal.

Difficulty: Easy

People + Resources Required:

❑ Sales Management

Successful salespeople structure meetings in a way that ensures that they stay in control, maintain rapport with the prospect, and maintain velocity through the sales process.

There are many ways to structure meetings, depending on your company's sales methodology. In this chapter, we will use a framework from Triangle Selling. Feel free to replace it with your own.

Step One: Standardize Meeting Structures

Notes

Sales teams that have all reps use the same structure for meetings have more predictable outcomes. Codify the beginning of each stage of the sales process (fig. 13.1).

> *Triangle Selling Framework: P.L.A.N.*
>
> *The P.L.A.N. is a salesperson's blueprint for ensuring that meetings stay on track and opportunities maintain momentum.*
>
> > ***Pivot**: Move from initial pleasantries to the business at hand.*
> > ***Logistics**: What are the mechanics of the meeting?*
> > ***Agendas**: What is going to be accomplished?*
> > ***Next Steps**: What decision will be made at the end of this meeting?*
>
> *Salespeople use a P.L.A.N. at the beginning of the meeting and then use a Velocity P.L.A.N. at the end of the meeting, which then becomes the P.L.A.N. at the top of the following meeting.*
>
> *As a result, the salesperson and prospect are constantly in agreement as to what will happen today and what comes next.*

Figure 13.1: Standardize the P.L.A.N. across stages

P.L.A.N.	Discovery	Demo	Proposal	Closing
Pivot				
Logistics				
Agendas				
Next Steps				

Specific examples of how the P.L.A.N. framework is applied can be found at TriangleSellingPlaybooks.com. If your methodology doesn't have a way to structure meetings, check out chapter 8 of Triangle Selling for more information.

Take Action

- ❏ Determine the how you can be prescriptive in teeing up every meeting for clear outcomes, and next steps. for each meeting in your sales process or achieve a similar result by leveraging a similar framework from your company's sales methodology.

Traps to Avoid

1. Failing to standardize how salespeople structure meetings makes it difficult for managers to coach.

2. Skipping steps in P.L.A.N. will render the entire framework useless.

Keep It Fresh

- Managers must update quarterly ensuring that the playbook is consistent with what is working in the field.

14

ELEMENT: DEMOS + PRESENTATIONS

Note: *For simplicity, we will refer to any form of presentation to a prospect as a demo throughout this chapter.*

Goal: Strong demos create a compelling reason for prospects to buy.

How It's Used: All employees who perform product demos should master this element.

Difficulty: Medium

People + Resources Required:

❑ Sales Management   ❑ Customer Success   ❑ Sales Engineering

The purpose of a demo is to create a compelling reason to purchase a product. That's it.

A demo must be well scripted, like a movie. Meandering through a features and benefits show-and-tell does not create a compelling reason to buy.

> *The demo is not the culmination of discovery; it is the continuation of discovery.*

The salesperson who leverages a framework to orchestrate the demo is in the best position to ensure that a demo fuels the sales process instead of stalling it.

Step One: Preparing for the Demo

Identify what the salesperson needs to accomplish prior to the demo meeting using figure 14.1.

Figure 14.1: Preparing for a demo

Topic	Description
Slide(s)	At least an agenda that ties to the relevant pain uncovered during discovery
Product	What will be shown?
Discovery questions	What needs to be asked that isn't already known?
Social proof	What relevant customer story can be used?
Content	Are there useful diagrams to include?
Next steps	What will happen next?

Step Two: Running the Demo

Define the steps that must take place in the meeting (fig. 14.2).

Figure 14.2: The demo meeting

Activity	Purpose
Show how to find trade shows	Solve the pain of not knowing how to find relevant shows
Analyze the audience at relevant shows	Show prospect how to forecast possible leads by audience segment at various shows

Salespeople must plan their demo activity and tie it back to pain uncovered in discovery. Demos are not presentations, but rather a backdrop for a conversation. Showing features that don't tie to a pain articulated by the prospect is a waste of time.

Pro Tip: Presentation Framework

Triangle Selling Framework: S.H.A.R.E.

Here is the acronym to remember what's important in a demo.

- ***Simple****: The best demos are simple and easy to understand.*

- ***Highlight****: To create a captivating and persuasive story line, it's critical to be compelling from the very start of the meeting.*

- ***Acute****: Salespeople must demonstrate their keen understanding of a prospect's pain and focus the solution on the acute reason a prospect would buy.*

- ***Relevant****: It is essential that the presentation is relevant to the problem, the person, and the organization.*

- ***Engaging****: The goal is to more deeply engage prospects in conversation, which will allow them to determine if they want to move from their comfort zone to action.*

S.H.A.R.E. applies to demos, presentations, and even storytelling—like customer stories.

Step Three: Maintaining Velocity Post-Demo

Many companies have no plan for post-demo. The hope is that a prospect will be wowed with features and will "close themselves." Instead, the sales process stalls after demo, and prospects either go dark or into the black box of "internal discussions." To avoid stalling, create post-demo velocity with the framework in figure 14.3.

Figure 14.3: Post-demo velocity

Topic	Description
Next step	
Timing of next step	
People involved in the next step	
Agenda for the next step	
What happens after the next step	

Step Four: Pull Everything Together

Once the pre-demo, demo, and post-demo steps are all identified, pull them together into a demo framework, shown in figure 14.4.

Figure 14.4: Example demo framework

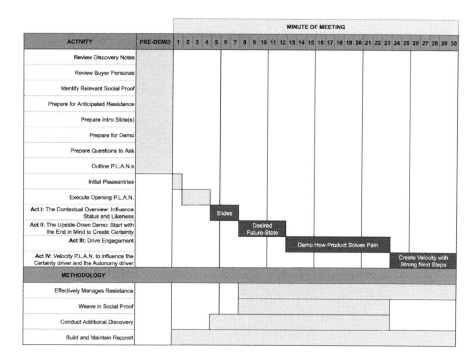

First create pre-demo tasks for the salesperson as a reminder to prep thoroughly on the right issues. Then create a GANTT chart that shows—in real meeting time—what activity should be taking place at that point in the conversation. These are guidelines and suggestions to ensure that a salesperson's meeting doesn't run off track, run out of time, or focus on the wrong area. Finally, so that salespeople understand that your sales methodology still underlies the entire demo conversation, identify under "methodology" where your sales methodology is specifically applied.

Take Action

❑ Develop a framework to prepare for a demo.

❑ Outline what will happen during a demo.

- ❏ Ensure that there is a plan to create post-demo velocity.

- ❏ Map out what an ideal demo for your company looks like, using figure 14.4 for guidance.

Traps to Avoid

1. Ensure that the sales team knows how to use demos to create a compelling reason for purchase and are not simply conducting show-and-tell.

2. Don't let poor demo meetings lead to a large number of stalled deals post-demo.

Keep It Fresh

- Update how demos are performed as major product releases occur.

- Observe post-demo deal velocity and make changes to how demo meetings are run if too many deals are stalling after the demo.

15

ELEMENT: CREATE MOMENTUM

Goal: Prevent the sales cycle from stalling by providing value to the buyer.

How It's Used:

SDRs: Keep leads warm who aren't immediately ready to speak with an AE.

AEs: Create momentum between scheduled meetings, build rapport with prospects, and mitigate the risk that incumbent competitors kill a deal at the last minute.

CSMs: Keep momentum between meetings with customers, especially with executive sponsors and other key stakeholders.

Difficulty: Easy

People + Resources Required:

- ❏ Sales Management
- ❏ Tenured Sales Reps

Step One: Tactics for Momentum between Meetings

Most companies have points along the sales process where momentum slows. Sales management must identify these points and use tactics to help create velocity. In Triangle Selling, the H.E.L.P. framework accomplishes this goal.

> *Triangle Selling Framework:* H.E.L.P.
>
> *Depending on a company's product and sales cycle, a salesperson can go a week, two, or even longer without talking to a prospect. Even with a clear next step set, what can be done in the interim?*
>
> *It's easy: H.E.L.P. the prospects.*
>
> **Highlight** *what was discussed in the prior meeting.*
> **Educate** *the prospect.*
> **Leverage** *your network to make valuable introductions.*
> **Predict** *the future.*

Figure 15.1: Framework for momentum between meetings

Tactic	Example
Highlight	
Educate	
Leverage	
Predict	

Specific examples of how to complete figure 15.1 are included at TriangleSellingPlaybook.com.

Step Two: Create a Cadence for Active Opportunities

After an initial demo or presentation, it can take several weeks or months until a deal closes, even under ideal circumstances. Competing priorities, bandwidth, and status quo create delays, so it's important to remain top-of-mind and reinforce the problem your buyer is facing to create urgency.

An example of a cadence for active opportunities is outlined in figure 15.2.

Figure 15.2: A cadence for active opportunities

Day of Sales Process	Sales Process Step	H.E.L.P. Step
15 (day after demo)	Demo to IT	Send champion X
20	Security review	?
35	Legal review	?

Take Action

❑ Create H.E.L.P. tactics and sequences for each team where it might be beneficial, including sales development, account executives, and customer success.

Traps to Avoid

1. In lieu of H.E.L.P., salespeople often send prospects messages to check in, touch base, follow up, bubble something to the top of their inbox, and so on. These are not value-adding activities and are not likely to move deals forward. In some cases, such activities can even damage rapport.

Keep It Fresh

- Review H.E.L.P. success stories on a quarterly basis and ensure they are shared with the rest of the team via the playbook.

- Identify the components of H.E.L.P. that are not being used and see if there are opportunities to try them out.

16

ELEMENT: TIME LINES

Goal: Increase win rates and forecast accuracy. When salespeople know each step that remains in a deal, they have a road map to fast disqualification or closing deals.

How It's Used:

AEs: Identify the target date for the contract to be signed and work backward to understand all the steps that need to be completed until the deal is closed.

CSMs: Similar to how AEs use it, but for upsell and cross-sell business. For renewals, work backward from the renewal date and ensure milestones are hit, or adjust course.

Difficulty: Easy

People + Resources Required:

- ❏ Sales Management
- ❏ Sales Engineering Leadership

Step One: Reverse Time line to Close

A reverse time line identifies the point at which a deal is closed and then works backward in time to today, highlighting every single action step that must be taken along the way (fig. 16.1).

Notes — Use either the contract signature date as the start of your reverse time line, or customer kick-off date, if there are a significant number of steps between contract and kickoff.

Figure 16.1: A reverse time line

A	B	C	D	E	F
Days after Demo	Milestone	If Trial	If No Trial	DQ Step?	Description
	Contract signed	X	X		
	Contract approved	X	X		
	Contract review begins	X	X		
	Send contract to customer	X	X		
	Contract presentation meeting	X	X	X	
	Contract sent for internal approval	X	X		
	Contract written/customized	X	X		
	Verbal agreement on terms	X	X		
	Trial summary	X		X	
	[INTERNAL] Go/no-go	X			
	Midtrial check-in	X			
	[INTERNAL] Activity review	X			
	Trial kick-off meeting	X			
	[INTERNAL] Plan trial	X			
	Send trial SOW (if necessary)	X			
	Send pretrial checklist	X			
	Agree to trial and criteria	X			
	Decide trial or no trial	X	X	X	
	Trial discussion	X	X		
	Demo	X	X		

Columns C and D in figure 16.1 account for a whether or not a trial occurs over the course of the reverse time line.

In column E, identify the steps which clearly define a commitment to disqualify the prospect.

Different reverse time lines are required for different market segments (enterprise vs. midmarket vs. small business) or products. An enterprise sale often includes:

- Demos or presentations to multiple stakeholders

- Detailed scoping to understand how the product will be deployed or service will be delivered

- Back-and-forth with the prospect's legal, procurement, and finance departments

- Security, compliance, and audit requirements

Step Two: Trial or Pilot Management

Create a more in-depth reverse time line for a trial or pilot to ensure that commitments are kept and momentum is maintained.

> *Triangle Selling Framework: G.R.O.W.*
> *G.R.O.W. is the framework used when a buyer starts with a trial, pilot, or a bite-sized initial purchase of a vendor's product or service.*
>
> ***Gather Resources****: Identify and mobilize political and other resources needed to expand beyond the pilot.*
>
> ***Roll Out the Pilot****: Officially roll out the pilot and obtain agreement on success metrics.*
>
> ***Organize a Communication Cadence****: Plan check-ins with various stakeholders over time.*
>
> ***Win a Larger Deal****: Work together with the prospect during the pilot, both knowing the ultimate goal.*

> **Notes**

Adapt G.R.O.W. or leverage the framework from your sales methodology to build out a pilot management plan, as shown in figure 16.2.

Figure 16.2: Managing a pilot

Stage	Activities	Expected Outcome
Pre-pilot		
Mid-pilot		
Post-pilot		

Find a complete pilot management framework at TriangleSellingPlaybook.com.

Take Action

- ❏ Define the reverse time line (or multiple reverse time lines) for your sales process.

- ❏ Formalize how you manage trials and/or pilots.

Traps to Avoid

1. Incomplete reverse time lines lead to sales reps skipping steps or "winging it," which will cause deals to stall or go off track.

2. Poorly managed trials and pilots require a lot of work in exchange for uncertain results.

Keep It Fresh

- Review the reverse time line quarterly and make adjustments if there are steps that should be added or removed based on recent wins and losses.

- Review the success of trials and pilots quarterly, and make adjustments to how they are managed if win rates are not sufficient.

17

ELEMENT: NEGOTIATION LEVERS

Goal: Standardize negotiations across the organization, thereby improving profit margins and mitigating the risk of unilateral concessions.

How It's Used:

AEs: Understand what aspects of a deal can and cannot be negotiated, and how.

CSMs: Same as AEs for upsell, cross-sell, and renewal business.

Difficulty: Medium

People + Resources Required:

❏ Sales Leadership   ❏ Customer Success

Step One: Identify Negotiation Levers

Sales teams must identify the various points that are negotiable and then outline what they are and are not willing to give up across each point. To start, list your company's negotiation levers and assign each one a weight (fig. 17.1). The greater the weight, the more reluctant your company is to negotiate on this specific lever. If a certain lever is non-negotiable, exclude it from this table.

Figure 17.1: Negotiation levers

Lever	Weight
Length of agreement	4
Price	4
Upfront payment	3
Support included	2

Step Two: Create a Negotiation Balance Sheet

We have outlined a negotiation balance sheet in figure 17.2. The items in column B outline what the salesperson's company cares about the most, while the items the prospect cares about are in column C. Columns A and D highlight the weight, which was established in figure 17.1.

Figure 17.2: Balanced negotiation

A	B	C	D
Weight	Your Company	Your Prospect	Weight
4	Length of agreement	Price	4
3	Upfront payment	Support included	2
3	# Users	Free months	2
2	Referral inside the company	Fixed price	3
3	Right to publish case study	Payment terms	4
6	Total	Total	6

In this example, a prospect is asking for a lower **price (4)** and **support included (2)** in the deal. Their negotiation weight equals (4 + 2) = 6. Our rep can now look to balance that request, instead of making a unilateral concession, by requesting **upfront payment (3)** and an increased **number of users (3)**. The negotiation is balanced since 3 + 3 = 6.

Take Action

❑ List your company's possible negotiation levers (fig. 17.1).

❑ Create a balanced negotiation table (fig. 17.2).

Traps to Avoid

1. If salespeople don't understand when or why certain points can or can't be negotiated, they will become frustrated when deals get pushed out or fall through.

2. Salespeople often "negotiate against themselves" by offering premature concessions before a prospect even asks.

Keep It Fresh

- As sales leadership and executive management makes adjustments to what is negotiable and to what extent, update the playbook so that everyone is on the same page.

- If it becomes clear that certain levers are more important to prospects, update their weight in figure 17.1 accordingly.

18

ELEMENT: CONTENT AND RESOURCES

Goal: Salespeople will have a single source for content that can positively impact the sales process, and they will be guided on how to best use it.

How It's Used:

    Marketing: Attract leads from the website and at events.

    AEs and CSMs: Educate prospects and manage Resistance.

Difficulty: Medium

People + Resources Required:

    ❏ Sales Management   ❏ Customer Success   ❏ Marketing

Step One: The Bray-Sorey Matrix

Utilizing the right content at the right time accelerates the sales process.

In *The Sales Enablement Playbook*, we introduced what Professor Sean Guillory has since called The Bray-Sorey Matrix, shown in figure 18.1.

Figure 18.1: The Bray-Sorey Matrix

Persona	Pain	Feature	Content

The goal of this matrix is to tie specific content to specific pain points for specific personas. Content that does not tie to solving a specific pain for a specific persona has little value in a sales process.

Pro Tip: Using Microcontent

There are two types of content relevant to sales:

- **Long-Form Content**: Multi-paragraph documents or slides that take more than a few seconds to consume. Examples include pitch decks, white papers, case studies, data sheets, and other similar documents.

- **Microcontent**: Words, phrases, and sentences that a salesperson can work into a conversation or drop into written communication.

Microcontent is the most effective in live selling conversations, yet it receives the least amount of focus.

Much of this book relates to microcontent. When given the choice between building out something complex, or simply surfacing the words, phrases, and sentences salespeople can use in conversations, focus on the latter.

Pro-Tip: When to Use Long-Form Content in the Sales Process

We know that when a prospect says, "Send me more information," that really means:

> *"I'm not interested, but I know that if I tell you that, you'll go into 'objection handling' mode, and I don't really want to deal with that today."*

While e-mailing content in response to the "more information" request isn't the right way to use content, there are great ways to use long-form content throughout the sales process:

- To explain complex topics like integrations or specifications

- To satisfy technical requirements, such as providing a security document for review by the prospect's IT team

Bonus Content: The Actionable Insights Map™

Most consulting firms closely guard their processes, frameworks, and tactics, but that's just not the ClozeLoop way. Here is one of our favorite frameworks that will have a monster impact on your organization.

The *actionable insights map (AIM)* takes a forensic look into current and former customers, the existing sales pipeline, as well deals that were lost in the past. The goal is to find concise and specific reasons why prospects:

1. Engaged in a conversation with your company

2. Chose to buy

3. Chose to stay

Salespeople then use these insights to find and close deals by leveraging microcontent that is hyper-specific to a prospect, their pain, and what will compel them to make a decision.

First, identify the attributes of prospects we want to examine. We have included common attributes for the AIM included in figure 18.2.

Figure 18.2: Common AIM attributes

Attribute
Persona
Industry
Use case

Next, identify your top personas (fig. 18.3), industries (fig. 18.4), and use cases (fig. 18.5).

Figure 18.3: Identify the top values for the first attribute

Persona
VP marketing
Head of events

Figure 18.4: Identify the top values for the second attribute

Industry
Computer software
Manufacturing

Figure 18.5: Identify the top values for the third attribute

Use Case
Increase # of leads
Improve event ROI

Now we are able to create an AIM template in figure 18.6 by combining the information we've gathered thus far.

Figure 18.6: The AIM template

Insight	Persona		Industry		Use Case	
	VP Marketing	Head—Events	Software	Manufacturing	More Leads	Higher ROI

Once we have figure 18.6 built, the next step is to populate insights and show how they are related to each of the identified attributes. For TradeShowMe, insights and how they relate to various attributes are outlined in figure 18.7.

Figure 18.7: TradeShowMe insights

Insight Label	Insight	Relevant Attribute(s)
A	Marketing VPs with lead quotas close fast	VP marketing, more leads
B	High conversion rate when head of events is a new hire into a newly created role	Head of events
C	Manufacturing companies that transport hardware are more cost-conscious	Manufacturing, higher ROI
D	Venture-backed software companies, especially with a recent funding round, are willing to invest heavily for more leads	Software, more leads

Now, we can take the insights we've uncovered and fill them into the AIM, while relating each to a relevant attribute (fig. 18.8). We will use the *insight label* from figure 18.7 to conserve space.

Figure 18.8: The AIM

Insight	Persona		Industry		Use Case	
	VP Marketing	Head—Events	Software	Manufacturing	More Leads	Higher ROI
A	x				x	
B		x				
C				x		x
D	x		x		x	

Notes

Additional columns can be added to the right so that for any insight salespeople have access to relevant:

- Case studies or customer stories
- Discovery questions
- Demo tips
- Prospecting tips
- Anticipated Resistance

AIM can be deployed in a spreadsheet or in other software. Either way, the key is the ability to filter by column, so a salesperson can drill down to the insights relevant to the attributes of his or her deal.

The hard part is coming up with a core set of insights, based on both data and credible anecdotes. Manually pouring over thousands of CRM records and interviewing salespeople is required for robust output. In the future, call-recording software will have meeting summarization models that make this work easier, but the technology isn't there yet.

Take Action

- ❑ Identify and index content that has been used successfully in the sales process.
- ❑ Ensure that content creators understand the differences between microcontent and long-form content.
- ❑ Develop an AIM.

Traps to Avoid

1. Identify when salespeople are providing content to prospects who say, "send me more information." This request is often a polite way of saying no, and salespeople who send information end up with stalled deals.

2. Creating an effective AIM is hard. Avoid letting the fear of hard work get in the way of progress.

Keep It Fresh

- **Long-Form Content**: Conduct a quarterly audit. Ensure that new quality content is added, and remove anything that is out of date or that is not being used to create pipeline velocity.

- **Microcontent**: Create a culture of adding strong microcontent. If people are not engaging, create contests and offer prizes in return for quality submissions.

- **AIM**: Assign a single owner to manage the AIM who updates it monthly, with a broader team review on a quarterly basis.

Notes

19

ELEMENT: REFERRALS

Goal: Generate consistent referrals by asking customers and prospects.

How It's Used:

SDRs, AEs, and CSMs: Create sales opportunities by asking for referrals.

Difficulty: Easy

People + Resources Required:

❑ Sales Management

Step One: Identify Referral Opportunities

Referrals are a low-friction way to keep the sales pipeline filled with quality leads (fig. 19.1).

> *Triangle Selling Framework: Connect the D.O.T.S.*
> *Referrals are one of the best ways to find good prospects. Our framework for generating referrals is D.O.T.S.:*
>
> ***Demographics:*** *What is the profile of the person to whom you want to be referred? Relevant attributes include the person's title, location, or industry.*
>
> ***Options:*** *What might a prospect be doing today to solve a problem instead of using your product or service? Bad answers here include a specific competitor or "nothing," but everything else is in play.*

> **Traits:** *What do your customers have in common? What do you know to be true about them that most people might not? What's your secret sauce?*
>
> **Symptoms:** *What are the signs that a problem exists that you can solve?*
>
> *It's not necessary to use all four points of the D.O.T.S. framework. The key is to be specific so that the person being asked remembers the context and will recognize the problem situation in the future. Complicated or verbose asks are quickly forgotten.*

Figure 19.1: Connect the D.O.T.S.

Category	Content
Demographics	
Options	
Traits	
Symptoms	

If your sales methodology includes a referral generation framework, include that in your playbook.

Pro Tip: Ask for Referrals

Salespeople, customer success managers, and executives should constantly be looking for referral opportunities. *Triangle Selling* sums it up well:

> *Some salespeople think there's a "right time" to ask for a referral. Maybe it doesn't feel right to ask a prospect who hasn't signed yet, or there might be hesitation to ask a current customer who isn't fully on board. We disagree with this sentiment and think that there should be no barriers to asking for a referral.*
>
> *Sure, prospects might hesitate to make any referrals before they sign, and customers might want their implementation to be completed prior to providing a public stamp of approval, but that's OK. If they say no, just as in sales, that's a "no for now," and it provides the opportunity to clarify when a better time to ask might be.*

Pro Tip: Measure Referrals

From your CRM sales leaders must be able to see the value of referred business that has been won, lost, and is currently in the pipeline. A few steps can be taken to drive up referral activity:

- Add "referral" as a drop-down menu in the CRM. Alternatively, create a text field labeled "referred by."

- Review reports on a monthly basis to observe referral activity by salesperson and by team.

- Periodically run spiffs for generating referral pipeline to reward the salespeople and sales managers with the largest number of referrals, as well as the most closed business as a result. Reward the activity you want to see more of across the team.

Take Action

❑ Create a process to identify referral opportunities.

❑ Create a process to measure referral activity and results.

Traps to Avoid

1. Companies that don't have a formal framework for generating referrals end up with few (if any) referrals in their pipeline.

2. When salespeople don't have a framework for asking for referrals, they will use ineffective asks, such as "Let me know if you come across anyone who needs better results from trade shows." When was the last time you heard someone at a cocktail party say, "I need better results from trade shows?"

Keep It Fresh

- Inspect the number of referrals generated on a quarterly basis.

- Create a dashboard that shows the amount of revenue generated from referred leads.

PART 4:
SALES DEVELOPMENT (PROSPECTING AND OPENING CONVERSATIONS)

20

ELEMENT: BUILDING A PROSPECT LIST

Goal: Standardizing the development of prospect lists ensures that outbound targets are of high quality, execution is efficient when they are identified, and the integrity of outreach experiments is maintained.

How It's Used:

    SDRs: Build their prospect lists

    AEs and Sales Managers: Advise the sales development team on prospect list development.

Difficulty: Easy

People + Resources Required:

- ❏ SDR Management
- ❏ Sales Leadership

Step One: Define the Market Segment

Define the segment of the target market (chapter 8) for which the list is being built. To do so, identify the list of attributes, as well as their values, as shown in figure 20.1.

Figure 20.1: Market segment definition

Attribute	Value
Company size	*500–1,500 employees*
Geography	*California*
Current solution	*Several Excel documents*

Step Two: Define the Persona

Define which persona(s) will be targeted (fig. 20.2). If your prospecting database requires specific job titles in addition to persona, ensure that all relevant titles are known as well. The goal is to group a large number of titles into a small number of personas for simplicity.

Figure 20.2: Persona definition

Persona	Job Titles
VP marketing	*VP marketing*
	CMO
	Head of marketing
Head of field marketing	*Director of field marketing*
	Head of field marketing

Pro Tip: Defining the Use Case

If your product has multiple use cases, segment the prospect list by use case. Messages must only discuss problems that prospects care about solving.

Step Three: Set List Goals

Determine how many prospects to source using pipeline math, as shown in figure 20.3.

Figure 20.3: Determining the size of the prospect list

Lead Stage	Conversion Rate (%)	Leads
New lead		*1,250*
Initial contact	*40*	*500*
Engaged in conversation	*20*	*100*
Opportunity created	*20*	*20*

Here, the conversion rate from a new lead to initial contact is 40 percent. For each *initial contact*, 20 percent *engage in a conversation* with the SDR. Of those who engaged in conversation, 20 percent ended up as an *opportunity created*.

Once SDR understands this math, they can work backward from the number of opportunities that need to be created and figure out how many leads need to be sourced. In this example, to create 20 opportunities, 100 conversations need to be had. To get 100 conversations, contact needs to be made with 500 leads, and to contact 500 prospects, 1,250 initial leads must be sourced at the very top of the funnel.

Step Four: Find Lead Information

Now, find the prospects' names and their contact information to create the prospect list (fig. 20.4). There are myriad tools available to accomplish this task. For highly targeted prospecting into large strategic accounts, manual analysis is required to figure out who to reach out to with which message. For SDRs with a large market, an automated approach limits research time.

Figure 20.4: The prospect list

Name	Company	Title	E-mail	Phone

Step Five: Load to CRM

Now it's time to load the prospect list into the CRM (ideally, this step happens automatically).

Once loaded, the SDR now has an easy process flow and a centralized means of managing the prospect list.

Pro Tip: Data Hygiene

Make sure that duplicates are removed during the data-loading process. Common places that duplicates exist include

- current sales opportunities
- current customers
- competitors
- previously disqualified deals

Automation tools usually handle this work on the fly.

Pro Tip: Time Management

SDR managers must keep a close eye on how much time their team spends doing research to avoid call reluctance.

Allocate specific blocks of time to conduct research—ideally outside of the hours when your SDR could actually reach a prospect live. Calendar these activities. This way, SDRs can focus their energy on the highest return activities and develop a consistent pace and call volume.

Take Action

- ❏ Define the process that your sales development reps and salespeople can follow to build a prospect list.

- ❏ Ensure that good time management practices are in place so that research is done within defined blocks of time.

Traps to Avoid

1. Asking someone to build a prospect list without strong guidance often leads to a list of random prospects that may or may not be in your target market.

2. An SDR is only as good as his or her prospect list. Every minute spent chasing a prospect that is not a target persona within their target market is wasted.

3. Ensure SDRs don't hide behind research activity. Strong time management practices mitigate the risk that people won't hit their goals because of research-related excuses.

Keep It Fresh

- Update this element based on new tools added to the tech stack and new tactics that have been found to be successful.

- Review how top-performing SDRs are building their prospect lists, and ensure that the most effective practices are included in the playbook for others to utilize.

21

ELEMENT: OUTBOUND PROSPECTING

Goal: Increase the number and quality of conversations by standardizing phone-prospecting activity across the team.

How It's Used:

    SDRs: Outbound prospecting

Difficulty: Easy

People + Resources Required:

❑ SDR Management   ❑ Sales Management

Step One: Calling Framework

In this step, you will outline the framework for a cold call. We prefer frameworks to scripts so that salespeople understand the psychology of the conversation and are able to adapt to the individual without sounding like automatons (fig. 21.1).

Notes

Figure 21.1: Typical cold call

Segment of Call	Talk Track
Opening	{{Prospect Name}}, this is {{Salesperson Name}} from {{Company}}. I know I've caught you unexpectedly. Can I explain why I've called in 60 seconds?
Why are you calling?	
Why does it matter?	
What is your ask?	
Confirm next step	

Another option is presented in figure 21.2.

Figure 21.2: A generic call framework

Stage of Call	Goal
Intro	Tell them who you are
Value proposition	Tell them why you called
Ask	Ask for a meeting with the AE
Commitment	Get a commitment from the prospect

Step Two: E-mail Prospecting Templates

Successful teams leverage multiple playbook elements, as well as strong e-mail fundamentals, in order to build effective outbound prospecting e-mails. An example of this process at work is shown in figure 21.3.

Figure 21.3: E-mail prospecting template

Persona	JTBD	Problem	Social Proof	Action
VP marketing	Evaluate trade shows	Can't justify spending in terms of leads, reach, and partnering	Acme—one trade show reached their whole market	Join fifteen-minute web meeting for TradeShowMe

E-mail	
Hi John, Are you responsible for evaluating trade show investments for ProspectCo? I work with VPs of marketing who have been struggling to justify trade show budget in terms of potential leads, publicity reach, and partnering opportunities. In a fifteen-minute web meeting, I can show you how ACME Co., one of our customers, was not just able to quantify these numbers, but actually reduced their trade show budget with higher impact last year. Best, Dan	

First start with the persona and JTBD table you developed in chapter 6; add to this the problem statements relevant to that persona. Next use the Bray-Sorey Matrix (chapter 18) to drop in some social proof. End the e-mail with the action you are asking a prospect to take.

Example e-mails are included in the playbook at TriangleSellingPlaybook.com.

Step Three: Other Prospecting Tactics

Other prospecting tactics work well in different scenarios (fig. 21.4). They don't all need to be used all the time, but anyone doing prospecting needs be aware of each and must have the skill to execute on them as well.

Figure 21.4: Other prospecting tactics

Tactic	Use Case
Video	Make a message come to life with a video. Embed it in the e-mail, or link to it.
Direct mail	Send something that will elicit a positive emotional response from the prospect and call them afterward.
Social	Include a social touch during a prospecting sequence, or practice more advanced social selling, as discussed in chapter 24.
What else?	Be creative. Run an experiment anytime someone has a feasible idea.

Take Action

- ❏ Develop a calling framework.
- ❏ Develop e-mail templates.
- ❏ Add additional prospecting tactics to the playbook, as you see fit.

Traps to Avoid

1. Some people will push back at the concept of a "script" and will want to do everything their own way. Creativity is great if it's within the confines of effective principles and frameworks, but otherwise, it results in chaos.

2. New ideas should be based on structured experiments that follow the scientific method. Otherwise, it will be difficult to gauge success and get real budget for additional tools or head count.

Keep It Fresh

- Review quarterly and make adjustments based on what is and isn't working for the sales development team.

- Add additional "other prospecting tactics" based on new ideas or observations of what is working for other companies.

22

ELEMENTS: QUALIFYING INBOUND LEADS

Goal: Improve the conversion of quality inbound leads into qualified sales opportunities.

How It's Used:

    Inbound SDRs: Convert inbound leads into sales opportunities.

Difficulty: Medium

People + Resources Required:

❏ Sales Management   ❏ SDR Management   ❏ Marketing

Step One: Identify Inbound Channels

Get started by listing the top five ways that inbound leads are created, keeping in mind that more can be added over time.

1. _____
2. _____
3. _____
4. _____
5. _____

Common inbound channels include the following:

Direct Message **Demo Request** **Web Chat**

Free Trial **Case Study**

Step Two: Map Inbound Channel to the Buyer's Journey

For each inbound channel, identify where a prospect sits along their buyer's journey. Specifically, what have they done before this action, and what are they likely to do next (fig. 22.1).

Figure 22.1: Inbound prospects along their buyer's journey

Inbound Activity	Prior Action	Logical Next Step
Download a white paper	Identify a problem, or a symptom of a problem	Attempt to understand if your company can help solve a problem
Sign up for a free trial	Attempt to understand if your company can help	Take a self-serve journey to validate or disqualify your company as a possible vendor
Request a demo	Saw something (unclear what) indicating that your product might be able to help solve a problem	See a demo to validate or disqualify your company as a possible vendor

Step Three: Map Messaging to Inbound Activity

In chapter 5, we developed discovery questions specific to inbound prospects. Here, we map that messaging directly to the specific inbound activity they took, as shown in figure 22.2.

Figure 22.2: Mapping discovery questions to inbound activity

Inbound Activity	Discovery Question
Download a white paper	
Sign up for a free trial	
Request a demo	

If your company has multiple actions attributed to a prospect within a single inbound activity category, then take the additional step of filling out figure 22.3.

Figure 22.3: A deeper map of discovery questions to inbound activity

Inbound Activity	Specific Asset	Discovery Question
Download a white paper	White paper 1	
	White paper 2	
	White paper 3	

We often hear inbound SDRs open up their conversations with generic open-ended questions such as the following:

Tell me why you reached out to us here at TradeShowMe?

The SDR is trying to get the prospect to sell themselves. This changes when the SDR says

Typically, when a VP of sales downloads White Paper 1, it's because they're struggling with pipeline velocity and are unable to hold their reps accountable to conversion metrics. Is that what you're seeing in your business?

This type of question creates credibility and will create rapid rapport with the prospect. Plus, if the VP says no, the SDR can always go back to asking why the prospect reached out to TradeShowMe!

Pro Tip: Inbound E-mail Principles

E-mails to inbound prospects must be relevant to the inquiry and seek to identify pain (fig. 22.4). Buyers are no less skeptical just because they reached out to you.

Figure 22.4: Inbound e-mail framework

Persona	Inquiry	Problem	Social Proof	Action
VP marketing	TradeShowMe ROI calculator	Can't justify spending in terms of leads, reach, and partnering	Acme—one trade show reached whole market	Join a ten-minute intro call
E-mail				

Notes

Hi John,

I noticed that you downloaded our ROI calculator on evaluating trade show investments. Is this your responsibility for ProspectCo?

I work with VPs of Marketing who have been struggling to justify trade show budget in terms of potential leads, publicity reach, and partnering opportunities.

Could we schedule ten minutes this week to answer any questions you have and share how we're saving money for other VPs of marketing?

Best,
Dan

Pro Tip: Inbound Call Principles

There are two stages of an inbound call:

Discovery: Does the prospect have enough pain to make it worth their time to enter a sales process with your company?

Qualification: Does the prospect fit within your target market, at least well enough for it to justify your salesperson investing in a sales process?

If the prospect does not have pain, it's unlikely that they will buy, and it's very likely that they will waste a lot of resources on the path to not making a purchase. It's critical that SDRs figure that out first.

Once pain is uncovered, ask the qualification questions needed to make sure that the deal is worth pursuing and which account executive should be assigned.

Take Action

- ❏ Identify the inbound channels.
- ❏ Map the channels to the buyer's journey.
- ❏ Map messaging to inbound activity.

Traps to Avoid

1. Make sure that SDR success is measured relative to the difficulty of the actual work they are doing. Converting someone who signed up for a free trial is much more difficult than converting someone who requested a demo.

2. Prospects who download information or do other activity on your website are not necessarily "expressing interest." Ensure that SDRs specifically reference the action a prospect has taken that triggered the outreach.

Keep It Fresh

- Add new inbound channels as they are created.

- Review messaging to inbound prospects quarterly and make adjustments if certain messaging isn't converting leads to opportunities at a high enough rate.

PART 5:
ADDITIONAL ELEMENTS

23

ELEMENT: UPSELL AND CROSS-SELL

Goal: Increase revenue by creating a process to increase lifetime value (LTV) of each customer.

How It's Used:

AEs: Engage upsell and cross-sell opportunities where AEs are responsible for this effort.

CSMs & AMs: Identify upsell and cross-sell opportunities, and engage them.

Difficulty: Hard

People + Resources Required:

- ❏ Sales Management
- ❏ Customer Success
- ❏ Customer Support
- ❏ Account Management
- ❏ Marketing

Step One: Identifying Characteristics

Identifying the upsell and cross-sell opportunities within your current customer base isn't rocket science. This activity often goes overlooked because the focus is on new business, but the sales function of an organization doesn't end there. In fact, we have many clients, who upon analysis, realize that they have 70 percent or more of their annual revenue from existing customers. Retention and growth areas are as important as new sales in ensuring that revenue targets meet projections.

Typical characteristics include

High User Engagement **Strong Satisfaction Scores**

Increasing Utilization **Discussing Pain with Success Rep**

Multiple Departments or Divisions **Support Tickets Solvable by Existing Products**

Start by listing signals that indicate an upsell or cross-sell opportunity, keeping in mind that more can be added over time.

1. _____
2. _____
3. _____
4. _____
5. _____

Step Two: Build a List

Once you have identified the characteristics that indicate a potential upsell or cross-sell opportunity, it is easy to build an initial list of target customers (both companies and contacts) to pursue.

Taking your list to individual customer success and account management reps is a great first place to get anecdotal information about where these opportunities exist today. Relying on this approach exclusively, however, is neither practical nor functional. To systemize the ongoing compilation of this list, fields must be added to your CRM, and they must be used by customer success, or the customer success and support technology stack must otherwise report on these indications. In either case, a searchable field that then populates a report is necessary to make this a process and not an event.

In the absence of a customer success or support technology stack, reps must be held responsible for a monthly knowledge transfer that is prioritized at the same level as a customer health score or customer review.

Step Three: Get a Conversation

Develop and deliver messaging based upon the characteristics you have established, using the same methodology you employed for outbound prospecting calls and e-mails. Examples are in Figures 23.1 and 23.2.

Figure 23.1: Upsell or cross-sell phone call

Persona	Problem	Social Proof	Action
CFO	Budget oversight of event participation	ACME CFO now able to evaluate cost vs. revenue	Ten-minute call for a demo using CustomerCo's data.

Phone Call	

after pleasantries

Jane, I can explain why I've called in about sixty seconds. Would that be OK?

I am working with CFOs of existing customers who have been struggling in the past to correlate event participation with revenue growth in a consistent and fair manner. Is that something that you are responsible for?

The CFO at ACME is another customer of ours in the A.I. space, and has begun using our event analysis tool to do just that in collaboration with marketing. They have found event expenses lowered by 23 percent, while revenue associated with events is up 33 percent. Would you have twenty minutes this week for me to show you how he's doing it?

Figure 23.2: Upsell or cross-sell e-mail

Persona	Problem	Social Proof	Action
CFO	Budget oversight of event participation	ACME CFO now able to evaluate cost vs. revenue	Ten-minute call for a demo using CustomerCo's data.

	E-mail	

Jane,

I am glad to find that your marketing department is benefiting from the use of TradeShowMe.

I am also working with CFOs of existing customers who have been struggling in the past to correlate event participation with revenue growth in a consistent and fair manner. Is that something that you are responsible for?

The CFO at ACME, another customer in the A.I. space, has begun using our event analysis tool to do just that in collaboration with marketing and has found event expenses lowered by 23 percent while revenue associated with events is up 33 percent.

Would you have twenty minutes this week for me to show you how he's doing it? Please let me know.

Alex

One of the most successful techniques to regularly conduct upsell or cross-sell discovery is to schedule periodic account reviews. In this conversation, both parties can explore how to maximize the relationship.

Step Four: Conducting the Account Review

During thev account review, the agenda should be customer-focused, with a major part covering how to possibly expand the scope of the relationship. A sample agenda is outlined in figure 23.3.

Figure 23.3: The account review agenda

Agenda Item
Review the existing relationship
Discuss challenges
Introduce new ways to work together
Plan next steps

During this meeting, leverage much of what we have already built in this book, including:

- Discovery questions (chapter 5)

- Customer stories (chapter 9)

- Resistance management (chapter 10)

- Personas (chapter 6)

- Competitive battlecards (chapter 11)

Take Action

- ❏ Identify characteristics of upsell and cross-sell opportunities.

- ❏ Develop the process to build a list of prospects.

- ❏ Develop phone and e-mail scripts to use when prospecting for upsell and cross-sell opportunities.

- ❏ Develop a process for conducting account reviews with current customers.

Traps to Avoid

1. Failure to conduct discovery on upsell or cross-sell opportunities will lead to smaller deals.

2. Some companies hire CSMs who do not want to sell and are simply interested in managing relationships. Ensure that the customer success hiring process aligns with the upsell and cross-sell goals of the organization.

Keep It Fresh

- Review quarterly and make adjustments.

- Listen to some recordings of account review meetings to observe what is working and what is not.

Notes

24

ELEMENT: SOCIAL PLAYS

Goal: Develop an omnichannel brand to reach prospects where they are.

How It's Used:

SDRs: Create brand awareness with prospects.

AEs: Create brand awareness with prospects, and execute H.E.L.P. sequences.

CSMs: Build rapport with upsell and cross-sell prospects, and execute H.E.L.P. sequences.

Difficulty: Medium

People + Resources Required:

- ❑ Sales Management
- ❑ Customer Success Leadership
- ❑ Digital Marketing

Pro Tip: Social Profile Audit

Social media profiles act as a form of inbound marketing. When a buyer visits a well-constructed profile, they better understand what the salesperson does, for whom, and how he or she might be able to help them.

At a minimum, the profile should include:

1. A professional image or graphics that helps the profile to stand out

2. Clarity regarding the primary problem(s) the person solves for customers

3. A call-to-action to engage or a top-of-funnel content offer (white paper, case study etc.)

Step One: Audience Building

Social selling involves creating original content, sharing the relevant content of others, and engaging in discussions around a topic. For this activity to be effective, your salespeople need an audience, which is composed of connections, followers, and other folks who are able to see the salesperson's activity. The larger and more relevant the audience, the more impactful their social activity will become. Here's how you help.

Take the personas that you developed in chapter 6 and designate their priority in audience development (fig. 24.1). You may add additional personas here to increase your audience to include those who would be in your target persona's circle of influence, relevant social media "influencers" who can help share your message, existing customers, and others. Get creative here—just be sure to prioritize so that efforts produce results.

Figure 24.1: Prioritizing personas to include in social audience

Persona	Priority
Persona 1	*High*
Persona 2	*Medium*
Persona 3	*Low*
Persona 4	*Low*

Once you have prioritized your personas, the salesperson will need to add them to their audience by connecting or inspiring the target to follow their posts and activity.

> **Notes**

Figure 24.2 outlines tactics used to build an audience and allows salespeople to set goals. Relative impact is included to indicate that an inbound connection from someone who likes what someone wrote will be stronger than a random outbound connection with no prior interaction. The former looks like networking, and the latter might look like spam.

Figure 24.2: Building an audience

Tactic	Relative Impact	Goal (Connects per Month)
Receive inbound connection requests from relevant posts and comments	High	
Outbound connection request after person likes or comments on a post or comment	Medium	
Outbound connection request with no prior interaction	Low	

Step Two: Audience Engagement

Sharing compelling content increases the salesperson's reach and relevance as a trusted source of quality information. Some connections and followers will engage with posts and activity by liking, commenting, and sharing it with their own audience.

The more relevant content is to specific personas, the greater the engagement will be. Use figure 24.3 to determine what type of content is relevant to each persona, and set engagement goals as well.

Figure 24.3: Identify engaging content for different audiences

Audience Persona	Type of Content	Expected Engagement

Step Three: Build Your Campaigns

Social activities must be planned in advance and run in campaigns in order to be adequately measured and cohesive. Figure 24.4 shows a partial social campaign for an upcoming webinar.

Figure 24.4: A simple social campaign

Example: Webinar Campaign		
Date	**Activity**	**Goal**
February 7th	*Text post about problem webinar discusses*	*100 likes and 20 comments*
February 8th	*Post about webinar + link*	*20 webinar signups, 50 likes, and 15 comments*
February 9th		

When creating social media activity, make it relevant to the audience and compelling. For example, consider the two following social posts:

> *Click below to see our latest research paper on why sales teams need better prospect data.*

OR

> *Does your sales team spend a lot of their day calling wrong numbers and cleaning up dirty data in the CRM? Click below for some possible solutions.*

The latter is certain to generate more relevant activity.

Take Action

- ❏ Conduct a social profile audit for all employees.
- ❏ Develop a strategy for employees to use social media to build and engage audiences.
- ❏ Create a framework for employees to build social campaigns.

Traps to Avoid

1. Salespeople can waste lots of time social selling, so time-box all social activities.

2. Too much self-promotional activity turns off the audience, so ensure that it's kept to a minimum.

Keep It Fresh

- Conduct a quarterly review of social selling effectiveness, and update this section based on learnings.

- Observe what social trends are working for others, and adapt them for your company's use.

25

ELEMENT: TRADE SHOWS AND CONFERENCES

Goal: In-person events yield stronger results when all employees at the event have and execute a plan.

How It's Used:

    Marketing Team: Create alignment between sales and marketing around events.

    SDRs: Create meetings for AEs with prospects before, during, or after events.

    AEs: Increase their effectiveness before, during, and after events.

Difficulty: Medium

People + Resources Required:

- ❏ Sales Management ❏ Field Marketing ❏ SDR Management

Step One: Set Goals

For each event, set the overall company goals and then break them down by individual attendee. Who are you trying to meet?

    New prospects?
    Existing prospects?
    Existing customers?

Partners?
Other people?

Get started by listing the types of people your salespeople will meet at the event.

1. _____

2. _____

3. _____

4. _____

5. _____

Next, take these answers and set quantitative goals (fig. 25.1).

Figure 25.1: Event goals

Meeting Type	Target Number of Meetings

Replicate figure 25.1 for each relevant person. Keep in mind that topics such as meeting new prospects might be as simple as exchanging business cards and a few words.

Step Two: Develop Messaging

Everyone attending the event should be conversant in persona-based messaging (chapter 6) and discovery questions (chapter 5).

Begin by developing event-specific messaging. Figure 25.2 outlines what people will say when prospects approach them at the booth in different circumstances.

Figure 25.2: Booth-based messaging

Message Type	Message
Opening line	
Passing a conversation to a colleague	
Short demo script	
Long demo script	
Response to "what do you do?"	
Response to "I'm not interested."	
Scheduling a next step	

If everyone on the team is aligned on each of these points, the booth will generate leads.

Messaging for when salespeople are away from the booth is outlined in figure 25.3.

Figure 25.3: Non-booth-based messaging

Message Type	Message
Opening line	
Response to "what do you do?"	
Response to "I'm not interested."	
Scheduling a next step	

These frameworks ensure that employees remain on-message at all times and drive goal attainment for the event.

Step Three: Plan Calendars for the Event

Between the financial investment and the opportunity cost of having sales people away from their desks, events are very expensive. To get the

Figure 25.4: Plan individual activity

Date	Time	Activity	Attendee(s)	Goal(s)

most return on your investment, ensure that people manage their time well during the event (fig. 25.4).

Capture everything. From morning "fun runs" to event-associated happy hour-specific goals.

Step Four: Convert Leads to Opportunities

A solid post-event plan will turn event activity into revenue. Before the event, determine who will follow up with which leads, how, when, and with what message. The specific tactics used will depend on your organizational structure and each team member's bandwidth. The important thing is that you have a specific plan.

Take Action

- ❑ Build out the frameworks in this element so that they can be used for each trade show your company attends.

- ❑ Define the metrics to measure the effectiveness of trade shows.

Traps to Avoid

1. Leaders who hope that their teams will "figure it out" during events are often disappointed.

2. Employees who are on their cell phones at booths or are otherwise distracted are unlikely to reach their goals.

Keep It Fresh

- Review after each major event and make adjustments as necessary.

- Coach individual employees on their performance after shows, and ensure that common areas for improvement are documented in the playbook and trained on prior to the next show.

Notes

26

ELEMENT: PLAYBOOK GLOSSARY

Goal: Create common language for culture, clarity, and accountability.

How It's Used:

   New Hires: Learn company and industry lingo

   Other Employees: Reference unknown terms

Difficulty: Medium

People + Resources Required:

- Playbook Team

Step One: Identify Key Words and Phrases

There are probably key words and phrases that are commonly used at your company, both internally and with prospects, which new hires have never heard before. Start the glossary element by creating a long list of these words and phrases by asking the following:

   Managers: What words and phrases create confusion for new hires?

   Tenured Employees: What vocabulary would help new hires ramp faster?

   Recent Hires: What words and phrases do you wish you knew on your first day of work?

Treat the creation of this list as a brainstorming exercise where there are no wrong answers. Consolidate and refine the list after creating an initial data dump.

Step Two: Get Agreement on Definitions

Words and phrases can have many definitions, but there is usually one most relevant to your organization. The person or team focused on developing the glossary should come up with the most relevant definition and get agreement from other stakeholders.

The glossary doesn't need to be anything fancy; it can be as basic as two columns in a spreadsheet, as shown in Figure 26.1.

Figure 26.1: A basic glossary layout

Phrase	Your Definition

Step Three: Build Competence

Beyond creating a glossary in the playbook, we have seen new hire ramp up time cut significantly with the introduction of flashcards and quizzes to ensure quick mastery of the material.

Use your company's LMS or another tool such as Google Forms to create a simple quiz to ensure mastery of the glossary.

Take Action

- ❑ Create a glossary that is seeded with terms that new employees will need to know.

- ❑ Ensure that new terms are added to the glossary on a periodic basis, especially by new employees during their first few days and weeks on the job.

- ❑ Create a quiz to ensure that new hires understand key terms

Traps to Avoid

1. Weak vocabulary can negatively impact employee performance, especially when dealing with prospects and customers who are subject matter experts and have a firm grasp on relevant terms.

2. Learning new vocabulary can be done quickly with relatively minimal effort. A few quizzes up front will be less painful than the prolonged inability to effectively communicate internally with coworkers and externally with prospects.

Keep It Fresh

- Update the glossary after each new hire class based on feedback on what people which they would have known then they started.

- Update the glossary with each new product release.

- Conduct a full glossary audit on a quarterly basis.

PART 6:
INTEGRATING THE PLAYBOOK

27

INTEGRATION: MEETING PLANNING AND DEBRIEFING

Goal: Improve the effectiveness of each sales meeting by preparing in advance using the playbook.

Good salespeople do not have a ton of time on their hands. Effective playbooks are efficiently used by salespeople in meeting planning. By leveraging the information that is known, along with multiple elements from the playbook and collective experience, deals become quickly disqualified (if not worth pursuing) or will move through a predictable sales process with a salesperson's strategic guidance.

Method: Personas in the Meeting

Thinking about who is in the meeting is key for preparation. First, ensure that the salesperson fully understands the buyer persona (fig. 27.1).

Figure 27.1: Understanding buyer personas

Persona	Reports To	Goals	Manages	Workflow

Next, make sure that any content that is prepared is relevant to specific pain that the personas in the meeting are known or suspected to have (fig. 27.2). Remember, content includes microcontent (words, phrases,

Notes

and sentences), as well as long-form content such as documents, slides, and so on.

Figure 27.2: The Bray-Sorey Matrix

Persona	Pain	Feature	Content

Additionally, ensure that salespeople are equipped with discovery questions that will resonate with the prospect based on his or her persona (fig. 27.3).

Figure 27.3: Segmenting discovery questions by persona

Persona	Discovery Question

Method: Relevant Use Case

Equip the salesperson with discovery questions relevant to any known or suspected use cases (fig. 27.4).

Figure 27.4: Segmenting discovery questions by use case

Use Case	Discovery Question

Method: Demo Product

If the meeting includes a demo, prepare the demo framework that will be used (fig. 27.5).

Figure 27.5: Example demo framework

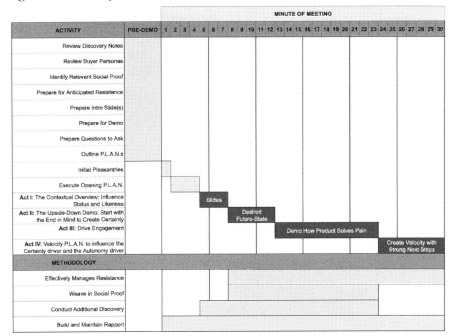

Method: Using Social Proof Appropriately in Meetings

Social proof is used in sales meetings to establish rapport, overcome objections, frame context, ask difficult questions, and conduct deeper discovery. The challenge with social proof is that it only works when it's relevant. Salespeople should prepare:

- Discovery questions to ask (chapter 5)

- Customer stories to use (chapter 9)

- Competitive messaging, if specific competitors are known or anticipated (chapters 5 and 11, winning zone)

- Tactics to manage known or anticipated Resistance (chapter 10)

Method: Meeting Goals?

The goals of the meeting are be defined in two parts:

1. **External** goals, which are shared with the prospect.

2. **Internal** goals, which are not shared with the prospect

To structure the external goals, ensure that salespeople make clear and get agreement on the decisions that need to be made at the end of each conversation. Then make prospects aware of next steps in order to create velocity from one stage to the next.

If the internal goal involves moving the prospect from one stage to the next, ensure that all exit criteria are met (fig. 27.6). Reviewing this information in advance of the meeting focuses the conversation and helps the salesperson to understand that they only need to "close" for the next meeting.

Figure 27.6: Exit criteria for each sales stage

Sales Stage	Exit Criteria
1 - Qualification	
2 - Demo	
3 - Proposal	
4 - Closing	
5 - Won	

Method: Post-Meeting Debrief

After each sales meeting, it's important to reflect on what went well and what didn't and to make adjustments for next time (fig. 27.7).

Salespeople can self-reflect for routine meetings, but they might want to engage a manager or other colleague (such as a sales engineer) following bigger or more critical meetings.

Figure 27.7: Post-meeting debrief scorecard

Category	Feedback
Persona and/or use case plan	
Discovery questions	
Demo execution	
Social proof	
Goals	

Take Action

- ❏ Customize the pre-meeting planning document to fit your sales process.

- ❏ Integrate pre-meeting planning into your CRM or note-taking application.

- ❏ Create a post-meeting debrief scorecard that a salesperson can use by himself or herself or with a colleague to reflect on what went well and what didn't.

- ❏ Ensure that sales managers are holding new and underperforming reps accountable for completing their pre-meeting planning and post-meeting debrief documents.

Traps to Avoid

1. Failure to plan increases the risk that winnable deals will not be won.

2. Lack of preparation makes continuous improvement and measuring effectiveness impossible.

3. Failure to reflect on meetings reduces a salesperson's ability to improve his or her performance.

Keep It Fresh

- Sales managers should watch out for opportunities to improve pre-meeting planning activities and update these frameworks accordingly.

- As new hires begin to have their first meetings, opportunities should be identified to strengthen pre-meeting planning and post-meeting debrief in order to further accelerate onboarding.

28

INTEGRATION: DEPLOYMENT AND CONTINUOUS IMPROVEMENT

Method: Deployment

Throughout the previous chapters, we have established guidelines to create quality content. Now it's time to think about how the playbook will deployed.

Based on our experience, the four most important attributes of a sales playbook are:

Content Quality: Is it concise, specific, and accurate?

Content Relevance: Is the content relevant to selling conversations, and activities?

Impact: Does using the playbook drive the metrics (such as OKR or KPI) that your organization measures?

User Experience: Is it easy for people to find what they need? Do they come back?

For small teams that sell one product to a defined market, the four points above can be satisfied with a playbook deployed in a spreadsheet, where each playbook element is a tab, and a linked table of contents is included on the first tab for easy navigation.

Organizations with more complexity require additional software to meet these goals. Playbook software is uniquely helpful at helping manage content quality and creating a better user experience, by hiding irrelevant information and making things easy to find through both browse and search capabilities. Analytics provide the admin with clarity on what is being used, when, by whom, and where there are blind spots. Playbook software also allows for a curated platform of useful information, eliminating hidden gems, approval bottlenecks, and misguided top-down messaging and process.

No one deployment option will work for everyone, so explore your options and see what best satisfies the above criteria for your organization. A word of caution, AGAIN:

> *Do not launch your playbook in a word processing document or in slides. It will fail. These formats are not dynamic, make collaboration and navigation difficult, discourage a feedback loop, forestall iteration, and* **will be useless in 90 days**.

Pro Tip: When Is the Playbook "Done?"

The playbook is a living resource, and therefore is never finished. There is a natural inclination to keep the playbook in development until it's "done," but the reality is that salespeople will get more out of a "good but not perfect" playbook than they will out of one that doesn't exist.

"The perfect is the enemy of the good." (usually attributed to Voltaire c. 1760)

Step One: Kickoff

The last steps prior to giving the team access to the playbook is to plan its rollout, as well as how its momentum will be maintained over time.

We recommend the following process:

1. Get as many people as possible in a room or on a web demo for a high-level walk through of the playbook. The person leading the playbook initiative should give specific examples of how it will be used, and the executive sponsor should talk about the organization's commitment to making the playbook a success.

2. Give people access to the playbook ASAP following the kickoff. No more than a day or two.

Notes

3. Provide a two-to-five minute walk-through video to all playbook users that shows a couple of use cases, as well as any other information they will need.

4. Schedule weekly office hours for people to ask questions about the playbook. If topics come up that could be useful to others, summarize key findings from the office hours and distribute them to the team.

Pro Tip: Signs the Playbook Is Succeeding or Failing

A key indication that a playbook is failing is poor user engagement. If sales reps are not using the playbook, that's a sign that something is wrong. Figure 28.1 outlines different signals that indicate if a playbook is failing or not.

Figure 28.1: Signs that a playbook is succeeding or failing

Category	Good Sign	Bad Sign
User experience	Everything I need is easy to find and easy to consume	• It's easier to [do something other than using the playbook] • Looking for what I need isn't worth the hassle
Information quality	Almost everything is up to date	• I don't trust it • [Element] is out of date
Culture	It's helpful how people collaborate around the playbook and are always adding helpful information	• [Person] still hasn't made the updates they promised • I don't have time to add anything new to the playbook • Perfection is getting in the way of progress
Managers	Integrate the playbook into team meetings and 1-1s	• Do not utilize the playbook with their teams • Do not encourage people to contribute content.
Senior reps	I've been selling for twenty years and still rely on the playbook for [specific elements]	It has good information, but I don't use it.
Junior reps	The playbook makes me better and is an invaluable resource	It would have been helpful when I started working here, but I'm all set now.

Step Two: Continuous Improvement

Once the playbook is launched, it's critical that each element is periodically reviewed and updated. One important thing to have is a playbook road map, as shown in figure 28.2.

Figure 28.2: The playbook road map

Opportunity	Target Date	Owner

In order to continuously drive success with the playbook, our recommendations include the following:

- **Assign Owners to each Element**: One individual person should own each element outlined in this book.

- **Hold Owners Accountable**: Management and executive leadership should have a mechanism to hold element owners accountable.

- **Appoint an Executive Sponsor**: One individual, ideally the most senior person involved with the sales team, should be the sponsor of the playbook, and must ensure that it is used and continues to exist as a living document.

- **Appoint a Playbook Admin**: This person might be on the sales enablement team or could be a frontline sales manager who is responsible for the day-to-day operations of the playbook. They make tactical calls on adding or removing frameworks or key components.

- **Archive Outdated Information**: Information that is no longer relevant should not be deleted forever, but it should be moved out of the way of active playbook users.

- **Drive the Culture of Collaboration**: Encourage all employees to add to and comment on the contents of the playbook. Additionally, schedule a monthly meeting to review the current state of the playbook with sales managers. Invite the executive sponsor and sales reps who are power users for additional support and insight.

- **Formalize Continuous Improvement**: Schedule one to two week "sprints" to address playbook road map topics, or to respond to issues with the current playbook.

Now it's time to drive results. Let's go!

APPENDIX A: GLOSSARY

- **Account Executives (AEs)**: Salespeople who manage the sales process from discovery to close.

- **Audience (social media context)**: People who view social media posts and comments.

- **Battlefield**: The area of competitive parity where there might be different approaches, but similar results can be realized, regardless of which vendor a prospect selects.

- **Benefit**: The positive impact a customer realizes from the feature of a product or service.

- **Buyer's Journey**: The path a buyer takes from the point they realize they have a problem until they make a decision whether or not to fix the problem, and if so, how.

- **Call Reluctance**: Procrastination as it relates to picking up the phone and calling prospects.

- **CAUSE**: An acronym for emotional words to insert into a discovery question (concerned, anxious, upset, struggling, and exhausted).

- **Channel Partners**: Third party organizations that sell and or implement a company's solution.

- **Circle of Influence**: The relationships (people) an individual relies upon for advice, opinion, or information regarding their JTBD.

- **Cross-sell**: Selling a prospect a different product than what they had originally bought. For example, if a furniture distributor originally sold a customer office chairs, the sale of cubicles would be a cross-sell.

- **Customer Stories**: Specific real-life examples of how prospects have used a vendor's product or service.

Notes

- **Customer Success Managers (CSMs)**: The people responsible for the ongoing relationship with the customer after the initial sale. For simplicity, we refer to account managers (AMs) and CSMs interchangeably.

- **Data Hygiene**: The act of keeping data clean and usable.

- **Discovery Question**: A question that leverages emotion and social proof to uncover pain.

- **D.O.T.S.**: A framework for generating referrals. The acronym stands for demographics, options, traits, and symptoms.

- **Exit Criteria**: The requirements that must be met for an opportunity to advance to the next stage of the sales process.

- **Experiments**: A test to either prove or disprove a hypothesis.

- **Feature**: An attribute or characteristic of a product or service.

- **H.E.L.P.**: A framework to create velocity between meetings. The acronym stands for highlight, educate, leverage, and predict.

- **Inbound Prospects**: Prospects that initiate contact with a seller's organization via their website, or other means.

- **Inertia**: Resistance where self-preservation has paralyzed the prospect. This person does nothing, possibly because past failures and disappointments are replaying over and over in their mind. Or they might believe that they already own or understand what they're being sold.

- **Information Gate**: A barrier to information that was historically created when prospects needed to talk with salespeople to learn about how to solve their problems. Information gates have largely been removed.

- **Job-To-Be-Done (JTBD)**: The specific job that a prospect or customer needs to accomplish.

- **Key Performance Indicators (KPI)**: Quantitative metrics that indicate leading or lagging performance.

- **Lead Score**: A quantitative value associated with a prospect that indicates how well they fit into a company's target market.

- **Long-Form Content**: Documents such as white papers, case studies, slide presentations, and so on.

- **Losing Zone**: The features, benefits, and problems solved that a salesperson's product or service simply cannot effectively compete with in a competitive deal.

- **Marketing Assets**: Documents, webpages, images, and other collateral that are used to market a product.

- **Microcontent**: Words, phrases, and sentences that salespeople and marketers can use to communicate with prospects.

- **Minimum Viable Playbook (MVP)**: An incomplete sales playbook that can still yield measurable results when used by the sales team.

- **Negotiation Lever**: A point on which a deal can be negotiated, such as price, scope, length of agreement, payment terms, and so on.

- **Objection Handling**: A form of Resistance management, where a salesperson responds to objections raised by the prospects, ideally with either questions or active listening.

- **Objectives and Key Results (OKR)**: A performance management system that focuses on measurable goals.

- **Onboarding**: The process a new hire goes through as they start their new role.

- **Outbound Prospects**: Prospects that are initially contacted via a salesperson via a cold call, outbound email, or other prospecting tactic.

- **Persona**: The role of a prospect within their organization. For simplicity, several similar job titles are often grouped into a single persona.

Notes

- **Pilot**: A small engagement with a customer, usually paid, that acts as the precursor for a larger deal.

- **P.L.A.N.**: A framework to structure meetings and create velocity throughout the sales process. The acronym stands for pivot, logistics, agendas, and next steps.

- **Playbook Blueprint**: An outline of a playbook that includes elements and some structure around what goes in each element.

- **Post-Sales**: A broad term for the team(s) that work with a customer after they have bought. Depending on the solution, post-sales might include customer success, account management, customer support, implementation, project management, and so on.

- **Pricing Guidelines**: The framework for discussing initial pricing with a prospect, as well as discounting.

- **Priority Path**: A framework to identify where solving a pain fits on a prospect's priority list.

- **Product Launch**: The act of introducing a new product to the market.

- **Product Road Map**: A company's future product offering that has yet to be released to the market.

- **Prospect List**: A list of prospective customers.

- **Reactance**: Resistance to the sales process itself.

- **Reason (Triangle Selling)**: The Reason aspect of Triangle Selling provides the tools for the salesperson to utilize a method of discovery that will compel the buyer(s) to articulate and confirm their Reason for making a purchasing decision.

- **Resistance (Triangle Selling)**: Prospect Resistance appears as no money, no urgency, no problem, no trust, or no confidence, but each of these boils down to one of the following forms of Resistance: reactance, skepticism, or inertia.

- **Resources (Triangle Selling)**: There are seven Resources that salespeople must remain aware of in the sales process: emotional, intellectual, financial, political, technical, human, and energy.

- **Sales Development Representatives (SDRs)**: Prospectors who convert inbound and outbound leads into meetings for their account executives.

- **Sales Engineers (SEs)**: Presales technical resources that work alongside AEs for technical sales.

- **Sales Methodology**: The techniques and skills a salesperson applies to the execution of their sales process.

- **Sales Process**: The linear steps that a salesperson follows to shepherd a prospect from first interaction until they are eventually disqualified or become a customer. **Sales Stages**: The key steps of the sales process. An example of sales stages for a simple transaction include: qualification, demo, proposal, closing, won, and lost.

- **S.C.A.L.E.**: A framework for measuring rapport that looks at five drivers: status, certainty, autonomy, likeness, and equity.

- **S.H.A.R.E.**: A framework to share demos and customer stories. The acronym stands for simple, highlight, acute, relevant, and engaging.

- **Skepticism**: Resistance where prospects are suspicious of buyers, their products, and their companies.

- **Social Profile**: An individual's profile page on a social networking site.

- **Social Proof**: One of Robert **Cialdini's** six principles of persuasion, (along with reciprocity, commitment/consistency, authority, liking, and scarcity) which maintains that people are especially likely to perform certain actions if they can relate to the people who performed the same actions before them.

- **Stack-Ranking**: The act of ordering a series of option in order of importance.

Notes

- **Target Market**: The combination of customer attributes where a vendor is best suited to win. Also known as ideal customer profile.

- **Tiger Team**: A group of people that work together on a special task, which is often not one of their core job functions.

- **Trial**: A small engagement, often unpaid, that helps a prospect determine if a product or service will meet their needs.

- **Tribal Knowledge**: Know-how that is stored in the heads of employees and not readily accessible by coworkers.

- **Upsell**: Selling a prospect more of a product they have already bought. For example, if a software company initially sold a customer 50 licenses, the sale of an additional 25 licenses of the same product would be an upsell.

- **WIIFM**: "What's in it for me?" A question that many coworkers will ask (at least to themselves) before volunteering to help with the playbook.

- **Winning Zone**: The area represents the set of problems a salesperson's product or service solves more effectively than the competition (keeping in mind that the competition might include "do-it-yourself").

APPENDIX B: SAMPLE INTERVIEW SCRIPTS

These scripts can be used as foundational templates for interviews. Adjust them as necessary to ensure that you are uncovering the information needed in order to build a robust playbook.

Executive Interview

- Understand the teams:
    - For small teams: Briefly tell us about each person on the sales team.
    - For large teams: Briefly tell us about your sales organization.
- Tell us about your target market.
- What are your buyer personas?
- Show us your sales process
    - Where are you having success?
    - Where do deals stall?
- The product
    - How do we talk about the product?
    - What is our pricing structure?
- All up-front, land + expand?
    - How are we doing demos today?
    - Can you send us a demo to review?

- Customer Stories
    - Tell us your strongest customer stories.
    - How are customer stories collected and disseminated throughout the team?
- What's your tech stack?
    - Can we get access to CRM and call recordings?
- What happens in a pipeline review meeting?
- Are any of the following things we should be concerned with?
    - Reverse time lines
    - Negotiation levers
    - SDR <> AE Handoff
- What content do you have that you use during the sales process? (decks, ROI calculators, case studies, etc.?)

Sales Rep (SDR or AE) Interview

1. Tell me a little about your industry and what got you excited about working at your company.
2. Why do customers buy your product? (make sure they are specific)
3. How would you describe your target market?
4. What buyer persona do you sell to? What problem is each trying to solve?
5. What are the most effective ways to get leads? What strategies don't work as well?
6. What objections do you run into? How do you manage this resistance?

7. Which parts of the future product road map have you really excited?

8. How do you use content as part of your selling process?

9. How do you use the CRM?

10. What sales tool do you need that you don't have today?

For AEs Only

1. What's your favorite deal you've won?

    a. Tell me about that sales process.

2. How do you structure demos today?

    a. What works well, and where do you run into roadblocks?

3. Where do deals get stuck in the sales process?

    a. What do you do to keep them going?

4. Are there certain prospects you'll disqualify? Why?

5. What's standing between you and your next level of performance?

APPENDIX C: OTHER BOOKS WE'VE WRITTEN

If you like what you've read here, check out the other sales books we have written.

Triangle Selling

Fast growth is the name of the game for sales organizations. Long-term success hinges upon a sales team with core skills and tactical frameworks that drive repeatable results.

Regardless of existing sales methodology, market, and company size, Triangle Selling empowers salespeople, managers, and executives to quickly adopt the fundamentals necessary to fuel consistent growth within their organization, onboard effectively, and remain agile in an ever-evolving profession.

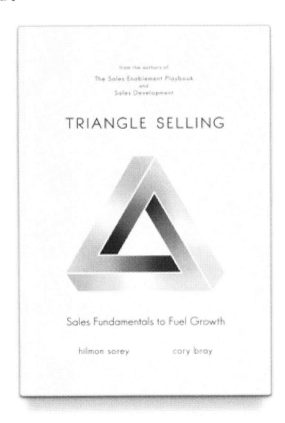

Notes

Like doctors, lawyers, and engineers who learn fundamental skills and frameworks to drive their work, this third book by industry veterans Sorey and Bray spells out, in practical language, the fundamentals of selling.

Contents:

Chapter 1: Introduction
Chapter 2: Why Focus on Sales Fundamentals?
Chapter 3: Communicating with Prospects
Chapter 4: Reason
Chapter 5: Resources
Chapter 6: Resistance
Chapter 8: Developing a P.L.A.N.
Chapter 9: H.E.L.P. Your Prospect
Chapter 10: Making Triangle Moves
Chapter 12: S.H.A.R.E. Your Demo
Chapter 14: G.R.O.W. Pilots to Win Larger Deals
Chapter 15: Connect the D.O.T.S.
Chapter 16: Proposals
Chapter 17: Running the Triangle
Chapter 18: Use Cases
Chapter 19: Getting Started

The Sales Enablement Playbook

In *The Sales Enablement Playbook*, we provide insights into creating a culture of sales enablement throughout your organization. This book provides a series of stand-alone chapters with frameworks and tactics that you can immediately implement, regardless of company size or industry. Whether you are a sales executive, a sales practitioner, or a non-sales executive looking for ways to impact growth, *The Sales Enablement Playbook* will help you identify your role in a thriving enablement ecosystem.

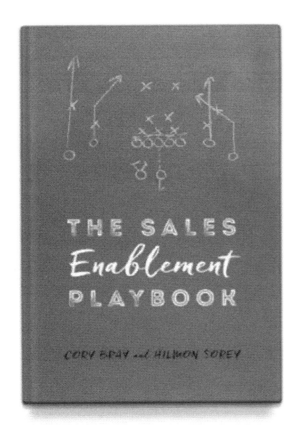

Contents:

Chapter 1: The Evolution of Sales Enablement
Chapter 2: Defining a Sales Process
Chapter 3: Onboarding New Hires
Chapter 4: Sales Training
Chapter 5: Who's Your Buyer?
Chapter 6: Product Training
Chapter 7: Tools
Chapter 8: Content
Chapter 9: Prospecting
Chapter 10: Closing
Chapter 11: Customer Success
Chapter 12: Hiring + Career Paths
Chapter 13: Channel Partners
Chapter 14: Sales Manager Enablement
Chapter 15: The Sales Enablement Position
Chapter 16: The #1 Sales Enablement Tool
Chapter 17: The Future of Sales Enablement

Sales Development

Sales development is one of the fastest growing careers in the United States. It is fast paced, often on the leading edge of technology, and people in the role have the possibility of making a ton of money!

Unlike accounting, medicine, or law, most salespeople do not study their profession in college. Instead, they are tossed into the fray without much training, context, or support and are left to sink or swim. This method proves neither efficient nor effective for the individual or the company.

Sales Development is specifically written for the job seeker or individual contributor who aspires to succeed in a sales development role, and beyond. This is your personal guidebook to the how, why, and what-to-dos of the sales development profession.

Written practically and tactically, this book shows you how to get the job, how to perform, and how to position yourself for advancement. Based upon ten years of teaching sales development representatives in the fastest-growing companies in the United States, this book will launch you on your path to becoming a rock star.

Notes

Contents:

Foreword by Chris Beall
Introduction
Chapter 1: Getting the Job
Chapter 2: Sales Strategy
Chapter 3: The Buyer
Chapter 4: The Market
Chapter 5: Your Product
Chapter 6: Working with Account Executives
Chapter 7: E-Mail
Chapter 8: Phone
Chapter 9: Social Media
Chapter 10: Other Prospecting Tactics
Chapter 11: Objection Handling
Chapter 12: Tools
Chapter 13: Time Management
Chapter 14: Core SDR Skills
Chapter 15: General Skills
Chapter 16: Working with Other Departments
Chapter 17: What Does My Manager Do?
Chapter 18: Mentors and Thought Leaders
Chapter 19: Career Path
Chapter 20: Figure It Out!
Chapter 21: Conclusion
Afterword by Ryan Reisert

APPENDIX D: ADDITIONAL RESOURCES

ClozeLoop is a sales management consulting and training firm based in San Francisco, California.

In each of our books, we lay out the very science, fundamentals, frameworks, and processes which we employ in our consulting engagements to generate successful outcomes for our clients. We believe in open-source sales intelligence and want readers to be able to immediately apply the insights from these pages without having to hire more employees or consultants. We love the ever-evolving nature of the selling profession, and it's our hope that other smart practitioners and executives will build upon the fundamentals discussed in this book and share their insights with us.

We welcome feedback and questions. Please connect with us on LinkedIn and shoot us a message.

The ClozeLoop Engagement Model

ClozeLoop engages with our clients through:

>**Sales Skills Assessment**: A twenty-minute online assessment where we evaluate the sales skills of a team across ten categories. We have specific assessments for sales development reps (openers), account executives (closers), sales engineers (presales technical resources), and sales managers.

>**Sales M.A.T.H.**: A guided executive-level quantitative exercise that begins with top-line revenue goals and then examines the health of the sales organization relevant to its ability to meet or exceed targets. We model Metrics (measure the things that matter—OKRs, KPIs), Alignment strategy (revenue simulations to clearly indicate where vulnerabilities exist), Time lines (cadence of review and performance reporting), and Horizons (long view of revenue targets with leading and lagging indicators and milestones).

Notes

Sales Enablement Assessment: A study of a company's current sales enablement ecosystem, challenges, and opportunities, including all departments that directly or indirectly impact revenue.

Triangle Sales Training: Multi-role on-site training for Triangle Selling.

Triangle Success Training: Customer success is the key to recurring revenue, and churn can kill growth. Triangle Success training is not just sales training adapted to customer success but, instead, built specifically for those who nurture customer relationships and are responsible for retention, renewal, and upsell of existing clients and customers.

Triangle Management Training: Frontline sales management fundamentals for Triangle Selling teams to develop accountability, coaching, mentoring, hiring and onboarding, and leadership skills.

Triangle Certification: Rigorous program for managers, sales enablement professionals, and independent consultants to be able to coach, develop curriculum, train, and reinforce Triangle Selling in their own organizations or with their clients.

Triangle S.H.A.R.E. (Demo) Certification: A rigorous program for companies in which product demonstration is a key step in their sales process. This certification increases conversion rate from the demo stage and creates velocity toward disqualification or closed business.

Triangle H.I.R.E. Training: Built for managers, H.I.R.E. training certifies those responsible for building sales teams in Hunting for sales talent, Interviewing effectively for selling roles, Rubric development for hiring success, and Evaluation of the candidate. When sales hiring is systematized, measurement and predictability occur.

Playbook Development: Develop and deliver a sales playbook that includes actionable sales tactics to ensure that all salespeople have an easy way to access the best plays for any specific selling scenario.

Playbook Audit: Review existing playbooks and provide both strategic and tactical advice on how to increase impact and create engagement.

Triangle A.I.M.: The Actionable Insights Map augments a sales playbook with the words, phrases, and sentences that a sales team needs to be effective in conversation with their prospect. Fortified with internal knowledge, customer evidence, external analysis, and solution positioning, this product puts relevant sales-ready language at a salesperson's fingertips.

Thank you for purchasing this book. We wish you tremendous success in your sales endeavors. If we can be a resource in your growth, we welcome the conversation.

Notes

NOTES

NOTES

NOTES

NOTES

NOTES

Made in the USA
Columbia, SC
15 January 2021